TEXAS SPORTS
H E R O E S

JORGE IBER, SERIES EDITOR

Also in this series:

108 Stitches: A Girl Grows Up with Baseball
Addie Beth Denton

Señor Sack: The Life of Gabriel Rivera
Jorge Iber

TONY ROMO

A TEXAS SPORTS HERO

JORGE IBER AND
RAQUEL IBER

ILLUSTRATED BY CONNIE NOBLE

TEXAS TECH UNIVERSITY PRESS

This book is typeset in Adobe Caslon Pro. The paper used in this book meets the minimum requirements of ANSI/NISO Z39.48-1992 (R1997). ⊗

Designed by Hannah Gaskamp
Cover illustration by Connie Noble

Library of Congress Cataloging-in-Publication Data
Names: Iber, Jorge, 1961– author. | Iber, Raquel, author. | Noble, Connie, illustrator. Title: Tony Romo: A Texas Sports Hero / Jorge Iber and Raquel Iber; illustrated by Connie Noble.
Description: Lubbock, Texas: Texas Tech University Press, 2022. | Series: Texas Sports Heroes | Audience: Grades 7–9 | Summary: "A story about NFL quarterback Tony Romo's journey to stardom, intended for young readers"—Provided by publisher.
Identifiers: LCCN 2022018207 (print) | LCCN 2022018208 (ebook) |

ISBN 978-1-68283-158-8 (paperback)
ISBN 978-1-68283-159-5 (ebook)

Subjects: LCSH: Romo, Tony—1980–, Juvenile literature. | Football players—United States—Biography—Juvenile literature. | Quarterbacks (Football)—United States—Biography—Juvenile literature.
Classification: LCC GV939.R646 I34 2022 (print) | LCC GV939.R646 (ebook) |

DDC 796.332092 [B]—dc23/eng/20220607
LC record available at https://lccn.loc.gov/2022018207
LC ebook record available at https://lccn.loc.gov/2022018208

Printed in the United States of America
22 23 24 25 26 27 28 29 30 / 9 8 7 6 5 4 3 2 1

Texas Tech University Press
Box 41037
Lubbock, Texas 79409-1037 USA
800.832.4042
ttup@ttu.edu
www.ttupress.org

This work is dedicated to our son, Matthew,
who has brought so much joy to our lives.

CONTENTS

PREFACE

T he careers of great professional athletes often have some unusual and unlikely circumstances at their heart. The story of Tony Romo is curious not only because of how he came to fame but also because of his family. You see, Tony Romo is the grandson of a Mexican worker who came to Texas as a young man to make a better life for himself. Tony's grandpa later moved to Wisconsin and there met his wife (she is Mexican American, born in Texas) and raised his family. Now, Wisconsin is not the first place that comes to mind when most people think about Mexican Americans, but Mexican Americans are a piece of that state's story, and the Romos are part of that tale.

Tony was born in California, but he grew up in Burlington, Wisconsin, a small town in the Midwest. He was a great athlete for his local high school. He lived a "common" life but did great things on the football field, the basketball court, the golf course, and in his classes. He worked hard to provide breaks for himself and made his dreams reality. This wonderful, all (Mexican) American tale is what you will learn about by reading this book. The story of the Romo family is an example of how many families, even those that include persons born outside of the United States, can, through hard work and effort, make their American dream come true.

That is not the only unusual or unlikely aspect of Tony's career. His time in the NFL ties in with two players in particular who would play major roles in his football life: one to whom he would be compared, the other whom he would replace as quarterback for the Dallas Cowboys' huddle.

Tony Romo and Tom Brady are both famous NFL quarterbacks. They are known for what they did on the field while playing for two well-liked teams: the New England Patriots and the Dallas Cowboys. While the years they played overlapped, their careers were different. First, Brady led his team to many titles, while Romo did not take Dallas to a final. Second, Brady came from a large, well-known school, while Romo played at a smaller one. Still, their experiences are alike in several ways. For instance, scouts believed that, coming out of school, there was little hope either of the two would make it big in the NFL. Their principal link, however, is that they both got their chance as starters thanks to one man: Drew Bledsoe. Brady came in for Bledsoe with New England after he was hurt in 2001, and then the Dallas Cowboys replaced Bledsoe with Romo in 2006. It is odd how one player was important in the lives of these two stars.

Tom Brady (still playing, now with Tampa Bay) has had a successful career. He was impressive at the University of Michigan, throwing for about 4,800 yards and 30 scores. His teams won 20 of the 25 games he started. In his final game, Brady threw for 369 yards and four scores as Michigan beat Alabama 35–34 in the Orange Bowl. Brady showed he could play at that level. Still, he was not picked until the sixth round of the April 2000 NFL draft. Other teams chose almost 200 other players before Tom had his name called. He never gave up, though, and when he got a chance to play, he did very, very well. He led his team to nine Super Bowls and 219 wins in 20 years. Not bad for such a late pick.

Tony Romo's career started differently. In the long history of the NFL there have been players who were not well known yet became stars. Romo did not play for a large college powerhouse; he played for Eastern Illinois University, which gets a lot less notice than Michigan does. But through hard work he was ready when he got his chance. Romo went from being unknown, not even drafted, to one of the Cowboys' greatest players ever.

TONY ROMO

CHAPTER 1

LIFE IN WISCONSIN VIA MEXICO AND CALIFORNIA

Tony Romo's granddad, Ramiro Romo Sr., was born in Múzquiz, Mexico, in 1933. The chief work there was, and still is, digging coal, silver, and lead.[1] Múzquiz lies at the center of Coahuila, a northern state that borders Texas. Its two main roads led north to the cities of Acuña and Piedras Negras. From there workers crossed into Texas and many went to San Antonio.[2] At age 11, Ramiro, with his mom and dad, went north. He said that it was easy to cross the border then. This was because, in 1944, Texans wanted Mexicans to work the fields to help the US during World War II. So, the Romos were just like many others—hoping for a better life.

When Ramiro turned 18 his mother died. His older brother moved the young man away from Texas to help him forget his pain. They went to a city called Racine, in Wisconsin. While it might surprise some, there is a long history of Mexicans in Wisconsin. The brothers arrived in November and Ramiro did not like the cold weather. After having lived all his life in Mexico and Texas, snow and cold were new to him. Ramiro did not think he would stay for

long and said that his "biggest hope was to learn English, work and return home."[3]

The brothers were not alone in Wisconsin, since many Mexicans went to the state in the 1950s. A report noted that they had been coming since the 1930s. Mexicans picked cherries and peas and then worked canning fruits and vegetables. They also planted and picked sugar beets. This was very hard work. Tending sugar beets is what is called "stoop labor." This means that workers were bent over most of the time to reach the plants with a short hoe. This kind of toil made backs ache. Also, the work did not pay much.

Many of the houses where the workers and their families lived were not well built and were overcrowded. Because of that, many of these people got sick as well. Then, after working hard all day, when these folks went into towns to buy goods, eat, or see a movie, they were often not treated well. In some places, they found signs that said, "We cater only to whites," which meant that Mexicans could not enter.[4]

Another problem for Mexicans in Wisconsin was that, as they moved from town to town to work crops, it was hard for their children to attend school. The fact that Ramiro was not able to get much schooling made an impression on him. He knew how important it was to go to school, and he would make sure that when he had children, they would be able to go. He knew that with an education, it was possible for the next generation of Romos to go far in the United States. As Tony began his rise to starting quarterback with the Cowboys, his grandfather noted, "I've always said this is a country of opportunities. If you don't get a job or an education, it's because you don't want to."[5]

About 10 years after Ramiro went north, another report by the state gave more information about the lives of Mexicans in Wisconsin. Things had not gotten much better. In 1961 there were almost 13,000 such workers. The way for them to get to their jobs was not very easy, as they often travelled packed tightly into buses or trucks, usually without much protection from bad weather. Then, again, the places where they lived were poorly built. The moms tried their best to make these shacks homelike for their families, but it was hard to keep out the cold. For the kids, the biggest problem was how to go to school while also working in the fields. Some farmers thought it was better if the children did not go to school at all, since the money they earned helped their families. Also, a few farmers believed, children were better suited for stoop labor than adults since they did not have to bend over as far.

The report also said that, by the age of 7, most of these children were one or two years behind in their reading. By the time they were 11, they were three or more years behind. One of the reasons for this was not because these boys and girls were not smart but because families moved every few weeks and children had to start at different schools over and over again. Even with all this effort, and with many in the family working, the Mexicans (most of whom were from Texas) made very little money—only about 85 cents per hour, which was about $710 per year. Just think about having to buy food, clothes, and other goods for your family on such a small income! Many people in Wisconsin and outside of the state tried to help better these people's lives, but it was a struggle.[6]

Because of this study, things started to change. In 1965, some churches got together to form a group called United Migrant Opportunity Services (UMOS) to work for better conditions. A year later, there was a large march to the capital city of Madison to make people aware of conditions for these workers. The marchers asked for better pay and housing. While it took another 10 years, in 1977 the state government passed a law that improved wages, hours, and shelter.[7]

With all of this going on, Ramiro Sr. did his best to build a good life. Soon he met his future wife, Felicita (her family simply calls her "Feli"). She was born in Robstown, Texas, in 1934, and her family went to Wisconsin when she was 12. In 2008, Ramiro recalled what life was like for him after his mother's death. "I felt very much alone [missing my mother], until I met her [Feli]. She is the one who most filled [caught] my eye." The couple married in June 1955 at St. John of Nepomuk Catholic Church in Racine.[8]

Ramiro, always a hard worker, held many jobs to support his family, which soon included Ramiro Jr. (Tony's dad), who was born in 1957, and an adopted boy, Mustafa John, who was born in 1967. The Romos' lives were busy. Over the years, Ramiro Sr. worked in a factory making sauerkraut in Franksville, owned a gas station, and owned a bar that he turned into a restaurant.[9] While neither Ramiro nor Felicita cared for the cold weather, they stayed in Wisconsin because they wanted their children to have a stable place to live. They did not want the life of a migrant for this generation of Romos. As Ramiro Sr. noted in 2017, "I wanted to return [to Texas], but I wanted to raise my children in one place, not to have them coming and going like migrants."[10] After moving back to Texas in 1980, he and Felicita ran two restaurants on the South Side of San Antonio between 1986 and 1989. The couple then retired to Crockett and have lived there ever since.[11]

While in Wisconsin, Ramiro Sr. and Felicita helped their people. For example, the pair worked with their church to set up two centers to help migrants. They also had a radio ministry in Spanish. The two continued to do the same kind of work in Texas after leaving San Antonio: helping those who did not speak English in local courts, performing more radio work, and guiding couples about to be married. Through such efforts in their home and community, they sought to pass along these beliefs to their sons.[12]

Ramiro Jr. grew up in Racine and was a good athlete. He played both basketball and soccer at St. Bonaventure High School. The fact that he went to a Catholic school shows how much Ramiro Sr. and Felicita valued both their faith and the importance of education. After graduating in 1975, Ramiro Jr. joined the Navy. He married Joan, whose maiden name was Jakubowski, shortly thereafter.

Joan attended Park High School and graduated in 1974. Ramiro and Joan had lived near each other, he at 410 English Street and she at 1701 Center Street. The two came from modest, hardworking families. In 2008 Ramiro Jr. talked about the values he and his wife lived by and hoped to pass on to their three children: Danielle, Jossalyn, and Tony. "My father never had much as far as education, but the things he accomplished just encouraged me to go out and be the best I could at whatever I was doing. A lot of the stuff that I have passed on and my wife has passed on to Tony . . . just basically our faith and our hard-work ethic. Those are all the things that we know."[13]

Antonio Ramiro Romo was born on April 21, 1980, while the family was still living at the Naval Base in San Diego. Although Tony was born in California, he lived there only a brief time. Ramiro Jr. retired from the Navy in 1982 and the family returned to Wisconsin. While Tony's grandparents still lived in Racine, which is located on the shore of Lake Michigan, Ramiro Jr., Joan, and their children moved around 27 miles west to Burlington, a town of about 10,000 people. The community has been described as "a Norman Rockwell scene" by one author.[14] What he meant was that it had the typical small-town feel of the Midwest. Everyone knows everyone, there are familiar places where children and adults go to eat and chat (and which have been around for many years), and there are just a few places to work in town. In Burlington, the majority of the people worked for the city government, at the local hospital, and at the Nestlé chocolate factory. It is this last workplace that gave the community its nickname: "Chocolate City."[15]

Here, Ramiro Jr. worked first as a carpenter and moved up the ladder of construction work. After many years, he became a construction superintendent: the person who runs the building projects. He did this type of work for more than 30 years. What Tony remembers is that his dad was always willing to play catch with him, even after a long day at a job site. "I don't care if he got home from 10 hours of work or 12 hours of work. He'd come home and I would have just been sitting there for four hours, so I would be ready to go. But he would say, 'Yeah, yeah, let's go!' And he'd go out there and get some gloves on."[16]

By the time the Romos returned to Wisconsin, the family was complete. Ramiro Jr. and Joan, along with Danielle, Jossalyn, and Tony, were back with their extended families. It was here that Tony, taking after his father's love for and talent at sports, would begin to make his own mark on the ball fields, basketball courts, and golf courses of his hometown.

CHAPTER 2

MAKING A NAME FOR HIMSELF IN BURLINGTON

Those of us who love sports and follow the careers of certain players often wonder how they got their start on the way to becoming pros. What was their life like when they were kids? How did they get interested in the game they play at the professional level? What role did their moms and dads have in setting them on the path to the NFL, the NBA, or the Major Leagues? Were they great at just this one sport, or did they play others? Who were the professionals who inspired them? Who were the coaches in their hometowns who helped them hone their skills? Finally, how did the athlete come to the attention of others outside of their hometowns?

These are the questions that we will explore about Tony Romo's life in this chapter. There are two important things to keep in mind about his days in Burlington. First, if one is a great athlete in a small town, it is easy to get noticed there. This is certainly a positive. However, the second point to remember is this: if one comes from a school that is not well known, it is more difficult to attract the attention of recruiters from large schools. The scouts for places like the University of Michigan (remember Tom Brady?)

often think about players in this way: "Sure, he is a good player. But he played at a small high school. What was the level of competition that he played against? Did he look great only in comparison to lesser athletes? How will he perform against players who have faced better foes at the high school level? Should we take a chance on someone like this?" These were the questions asked about Tony and his abilities.

While he made a name for himself in Burlington, when it came time to look for a place to play at the next level (college) not many schools were interested in giving Romo a chance. Someone would in the end offer him an opportunity, but it would certainly not be in the "big time" of college football. As you will see, it was the work ethic taught by his parents, grandparents, and coaches, as well as his athletic skills, that made it possible for Tony to play at this next level. He got an opportunity and made the best of it, just as Ramiro Sr. noted about life in his adopted country.

As Ramiro Jr. worked his way up the construction business over a 30-year period, he sought out a way to stay active away from the job. Remember, he was an athlete in high school, and it is not easy to forget the thrill of athletics. He found his outlet with the help of Joan's brother. Around 1986 the two went to Shoop Park, a city golf course in Racine. After his first shot, Ramiro was hooked. "I'll never forget the first shot I hit. I just laced a beautiful shot right down the middle. That's when the bug hit me. . . . I wound up shooting 74 for those nine holes." He took his first lesson two years later and has been playing ever since. "Once you start having success you want to get better." Indeed, he became such a fan of the sport that by the mid-2010s he became part owner of the Meadowbrook Country Club in Racine and worked with the Wisconsin

State Golf Association to get young people to play golf. As his dad began this hobby, Tony started to tag along and in short order he, too, was hooked. Soon, Joan also got a job at a course (although she did not care to play), and the locale became "a miniature daycare center at times." Eventually, Jossalyn also played golf (at the high school level).[1]

From when he was young, Tony took after his dad and was drawn to sports—many of them. He kept his parents busy, to say the least. In an interview with Graham Bensinger, he spoke about always being ready to play.[2] Season after season, sport after sport, Tony wanted to compete. In a 2012 article by Peter Simek, the author noted that early on Tony played soccer (like his dad did in high school), golf, and basketball. It turned out that hoops was his best game (as you will see shortly). On weekends, Ramiro and Tony would often drive "from town to town in rural Wisconsin, looking for pickup basketball and soccer games." Then, after competing in such events, Tony turned to "video games, poker, or chess—anything to stay in competition—in the basements of his friends' homes."[3] He was so wired about playing, he said, that if he had been the first child in the family instead of the third, Ramiro and Joan might not have had other children. From the get-go, it was tough to keep up with Tony. By age 11 he had become a local Little League All-Star, first in 1991 and again in 1992.[4] Although he had success on the diamond, the baseball phase did not last. "He wanted to be a pitcher, but accuracy was lacking. He just didn't know where the ball was going," Ramiro said. "But as a catcher, he was [very] accurate."[5]

As the 1990s moved on, Tony's name appeared quite often in the Racine *Journal Times*, the paper that covered the news in that city and surrounding areas. In addition to his success in sports, an early mention noted that Romo made the honor roll in the last quarter of his eighth grade in the 1993–1994 school year.[6] While he did well in school, Tony was not above also having a little fun in the classroom. Romo's high school shop teacher, Bob Musgrave, said that he "always thought [Tony] was paying attention when he got there early. We sat at this bench on stools and he's looking at his knees. . . . Little did I know he had swiped the sports section from my table and was reading it during the class."[7]

Even before his freshman year at Burlington High School (BHS), Tony achieved notice via his abilities on the links, as he shot a 96 and finished in 11th place (in the 13- to 14-year-old group) at the Racine County Junior Tournament at Browns Lake Golf Course.[8] By the end of his first year at BHS, there was a story on Tony and his teammates on the golf team (they finished 7–4) that tied their success to the sway of the dads, who kept the players on the course even when school was not in session. Of course, Ramiro was one of the fathers mentioned. As team coach Bill Berkholtz stated, "The kids had a real good work ethic this year and I think that's in large part because they play with their fathers."[9]

Heading into his sophomore year, Tony received his first mention as a basketball player. First-year coach Steve Berezowitz's team was coming off a losing season (8–13), but there was hope for a better year in 1995–1996. One reason for this was that the team was strong in the guard position. While Romo was not the starter, his coach said that he "sees the court and runs the team extremely well for a sophomore." It would not be the last time that Tony's ability to "see" the game would be noticed.[10] By the end of that season, he earned Honorable Mention.[11] Just two months later, he earned first-team all-county in golf.[12] Indeed, Coach Berkholtz believes that Romo's ability to think tactically on the football field came from what he learned on the links. "He was so patient on the golf course. When he throws an interception, it's a golfer's mentality; make a bad shot let it fester or you can say that's done it's on to the next shot."[13]

There is one story about Tony's sophomore basketball season that has become a local legend. The Burlington Demons were scheduled to play the East Troy Trojans on the road. As the team prepared to board their bus to head to their opponents' gym, Tony was not on board. Coach Berezowitz's rules were that if you were not on the bus, you did not play. This was an important game, and Tony's play would be of great help. Where was he? As the bus rolled out of the parking lot at BHS, Tony was on his way—on his bicycle (it was a 15-mile trip one way). Remember that this is Wisconsin in the late fall or early winter: that means it was snowing. No matter. Tony knew that his coach and team were counting on him, so off he went. What had happened was that Ramiro, who would always take his son to school for away games, was coming back from out of town and was delayed by the snow. Luckily, Ramiro saw his son on his bike, picked him up, and then drove him to East Troy. Wisely, Coach Berezowitz made an exception to his rule. "We would have been dead without him. . . . We won in overtime." Ramiro was so amazed by his son's drive and grit that he started crying before Tony entered his vehicle. "Ramiro had never seen such want."[14]

We have already talked about how Tony got hooked on golf and his passing ties to soccer and baseball, but how did he become interested in basketball? Well, both Ramiro and Joan had a hand in this as well. The family put up a rim in their driveway when Tony was about six. The goal was set at the standard 10-foot height, not exactly an easy target for a youngster. They never lowered the rim, and Tony kept shooting. It took a great deal of effort and patience (noticing a pattern here?) to make baskets. Ramiro remembered that, after clearing away snow during the winter months, "the little guy would be out there for two hours and make two baskets." While working hard in the driveway, Tony also got hooked on watching videotape (this was the 1990s) of one of the greatest players of all time—"Pistol" Pete Maravich of Louisiana State University—and several NBA teams. Joan recalled that her son wore out three video cassette recorders (known as VCRs; you will have to ask your parents what this is) while watching how Pete handled and shot the ball. In addition to watching film, Tony devoured sports books. He particularly read and reread one about another great shooter: Larry Bird of Indiana State and, famously, the Boston Celtics.[15]

By his junior season, Tony was a leader for the BHS Demons, almost a second coach on the court. Since he was a point guard, that meant he had the ball in his hands often when the Demons had possession (this was also important on the football field, as you will see). Tony's job was to look over the defense his opponents were playing and come up with a strong plan of attack. This ability is often called being able to "read" the defense, and it is a part not just of basketball but also football. This skill would serve Tony well not only as a player but also years later, when he began his broadcasting career. Coach Berezowitz believes Romo had a set of unique skills. In addition to being a good shooter, he was smart at attacking defenses and was "so unselfish, [and] that really helps the ballclub. He's just a great kid; he always finds a way to make something happen."[16] The end result was that, at the end of the 1996–1997 school year, Romo was named second-team All-Racine County in basketball. He averaged 15.6 points per game and had more than six rebounds and assists each contest.[17] He then followed up by being named Player of the Year in his conference as a senior (he averaged 24.3 points and almost nine rebounds per game). Even more notably, he was third team Associated Press All-State.[18]

Now that we have covered Tony's exploits in other sports, what about football? How did he come to play this sport? After all, he is famous for playing for the Cowboys, not for playing in the NBA or on the professional golf tour. It should not be a surprise that Tony, with such a knack for competition, thought about joining the Demons' football team starting in the fall of his first year at BHS. Ramiro asked his son what position he was interested in playing; of course, he wanted to play quarterback. This should not be a surprise, given that, as a point guard—the player who handles the ball on every trip up the court—Tony would likewise want the ball in his hands on every snap on the football field. Just as he had done with Maravich and Bird in basketball, Tony set his sights on following and imitating a legend on the football field: Joe Montana. After the initial few practices with the first-year team, he was listed as the seventh-string quarterback and backup safety. Not much was expected from Romo but, as would be the case with the Cowboys years later, he would prove coaches wrong.[19]

To make matters worse, when it seemed that Romo might line up under center for the BHS junior varsity as a sophomore, he suffered a broken finger that knocked him out for the season. The injury took place during a preseason practice in which, witnesses say, one of the coaches (who was mad at Tony for some reason and wanted to have him "taken down a notch") called a play designed to "get Romo." The players on defense got a clear path to Tony (called a bull rush) as he dropped to pass, then sacked and injured him.[20]

By the start of his junior year Tony had moved up to varsity, but he was still not listed as the starter. In 1996 Steve Gerber became the new head coach of the Demons, replacing a local legend named Don Dalton, who coached BHS to more than 200 victories between 1969 and 1995. Under Coach Dalton, the Demons were very much a traditional Midwest football team, in the mold of coaches such as the late Ohio State legend Woody Hayes. In other words, their offense was based on running and controlling the ball. The saying by Hayes and others during this era was that they were happy with each play producing "three yards and a cloud of dust." Well, Gerber was of a different mind. He saw what was happening in the NFL and at the college level during the early 1990s: the game now featured more passing than it had before.[21]

This style of offense placed a lot of responsibility on the quarterback. It was his duty to look at the defense, figure out what they were doing, and come up with ways to counter it. In football, this means that the quarterback must read the situation and understand how the various routes his receivers are running can attack the defense. In football talk, the quarterback is going through progressions as he steps back to pass. If the first receiver is covered, the quarterback must know where the second, third, or fourth receiver is and throw the ball there. This calls for quick thinking and decision making, as well as avoiding defenders who are trying to tackle you. The typical quarterback at the high school level might go through two progressions. If a player can move beyond that (to a third or fourth receiver in the play), then he is on his way to becoming a star. Given Tony's time on the basketball court doing something similar, it is easy to see how this benefited his play under center.[22]

After the first game of the 1996 season, Gerber's offense was in trouble. The two quarterbacks in front of Tony combined to throw for a measly 12 yards in the air and a total of 58 yards of output. BHS lost, 15–0. Enter Tony Romo as starter. Gerber also moved another great athlete, Steve Tenhagen, to tight end. The combination would work wonders for the Demons in 1996.[23] The results were immediate in the second game of the season against Elkhorn. Tony passed for 308 yards, and two of his receivers totaled more than 100 yards each. No quarterback in the area had thrown for more yardage since 1984. Although the Demons lost, 34–14, Coach Gerber had found his quarterback. By the end of the year, Tenhagen and Romo would combine for 56 catches, 934 yards, and 13 scores.[24] The Demons ended the year with a record of 9–3. Tony finished the year with 125 completions out of 192 attempts for 1,851 yards and 26 touchdowns. He also made first team All-Racine County. Not bad for someone who had not played in a varsity game before his first start. Most important, Coach Gerber noted the one key skill that made Tony different from other quarterbacks, one that would help him get to the NFL. "He was able to see coverage. We tried to prepare him for what he would see, but it's still up to him to open the right window. He sees things that you almost can't coach."[25] Again, this is a skill that would come in handy for Tony not only as a player but as an NFL analyst years later.

Success in 1996 came with a price for BHS as Wisconsin school authorities moved them to a higher classification for 1997. Here was an opportunity for Tony to prove himself against better competition, but it also meant that, playing against larger schools (with a larger pool of athletes), the Demons would be overmatched. Still, heading into his senior year, he sought to do well and continued to have a great sense of humor. Once again, drawing from his video collection, Romo spent much of that year quoting from the movie *The Program*. Some of his quotes and actions were corny, to say the least. In one game, he ran out to the field on defense and yelled, "Starting defense, baby!" Coach Gerber thought that there was someone other than the proper player lined up at safety, and quickly removed his starting quarterback from the field. At another point in the season, Tony told his huddled teammates that it was time to "put the women and children to bed and go looking for dinner!" Another quote straight from the movie. Steve Tenhagen recalled that this was very much in character for his friend. "He always screwed around like that. Guys loved that. He's ultra-competitive but can still keep a sense of humor about what he's doing."[26]

Although his team was outmanned, Tony had an excellent season. During that year, he had his most impressive high school game, although it came in a defeat. On September 26, the Demons took on the Racine Case Eagles, year after year a strong challenger for state honors. The final score was 51–34, Eagles. But that was not the whole story. In this contest, against some of the best competition he had faced, Tony kept his team in the game. He threw for 392 yards and four scores. Also, he showed his toughness by taking a vicious hit from a Case linebacker in the third quarter. The impact lifted Tony off the ground, and he wound up slammed to the turf on his back. After having to come out of the game briefly, Tony returned and led his team to two more scores using a no-huddle (speeded up—in other words, the team would not huddle to call a play; that would be done at the line of scrimmage) offense. The game was out of reach, but Romo made a great impression. One of the coaches for Case, after watching the game film, said, "You knock a guy out, he comes back in, and he just torches you. . . . I think if he goes to a city [Racine] school, he goes to a high Division I university."[27]

That year, BHS finished 3–6. Still, Tony stood out and earned a place on the first All-State Team voted on by the Wisconsin Football Coaches Association. Quite an honor for a player on a losing team. While he threw for more yards, he did have fewer scoring passes. Still, coaches and reporters understood what he achieved against better competition. What Tony proved was how his physical skills matched up with his smarts. Coach Gerber said that Romo called audibles (where the quarterback changes the play at the line of scrimmage based on what he sees from the defense) "60 to 65 percent of the plays . . . and I'd say about 75 to 85 percent of them were the right call." As Tony wrapped up his high school career, Coach Gerber maintained that he was a complete package under center. "He's unique in that he just picks things up so easily. . . . Not just mechanically is he able to master skills like that, but mentally, he sees things that will help him mechanically." Pete Jackel, the reporter who covered Tony's career at BHS, supported this statement. He told Peter Simek that "he made a comment to me one time that I never forgot. He said, 'I just see things in slow motion. I just see it. I see the game well.'" All told, Romo threw for more than 3,700 yards and 42 scores over this time with the Demons.[28]

After such a career, one would think that scouts from schools at the next level would have been beating a path to Romo's door. That was not the case, however. Now came the critical moment. Tony had done well in basketball, so

maybe a school would be interested in providing a scholarship to be on their court. Football, in which he had earned the most acclaim and which he had come to love, might not be his ticket to a university. The Romos did not have money to spare, so a scholarship was vital. It was here that Peter Jackel stepped in and helped. You see, one advantage of living in a small town is that people know each other. Jackel, it turns out, was the childhood friend of a man named Roy Wittke, another native of Racine. Wittke, who played college football at Wisconsin–Eau Claire and coached at Montana State and Central Missouri State, was now the offensive coordinator at Eastern Illinois University (EIU), located in Charleston, Illinois. Wittke saw Romo play basketball and read about his results in football. He was intrigued.

There were two final hurdles to overcome. First, while Wittke wanted to sign Romo, he wanted him to play only football for the Panthers. So, any chance for Tony to play hoops at the next level would end. Second, Wittke had to convince his boss, head coach Bob Spoo, to provide the scholarship. Tony agreed to give up basketball and Wittke showed Romo's game films to Spoo. There were positives and negatives. The Panthers' head coach recalled that "Tony was raw . . . [but] what was readily apparent was . . . that he was a serious competitor. . . . What it came down to was I felt Tony had a good frame, and he would get bigger and stronger and worth the risk of a partial scholarship."[29]

The value of the offer was around $4,000 to $5,000. Normally, a football player gets a full scholarship, so the Romos would have to foot some of the bill. Still, this was the chance Tony wanted, and it would certainly help the family. So, he took the EIU offer and became a Panther. Little did Coach Spoo and Tony Romo realize what this small investment would turn into.

CHAPTER 3

A BIG CAT IN A SMALL JUNGLE, 1998-2000

When Tony Romo went to Eastern Illinois University in fall 1998, he arrived at a school that had a long history in football (since 1899), but that always played in the lower levels of the sport. After some good years in the 1940s, their teams had a long dry spell: only three winning years in the 30 seasons after 1948. One of those years, however—in 1978—they won the Division II National Title. The Panthers made it back to the title game in 1980, only to lose by one point.[1]

In 1981 EIU moved up one level to I-AA, and over the years made 12 visits to the playoffs. Unlike the larger schools, I-AA teams send division winners to a playoff to crown their champ. The NCAA (National Collegiate Athletic Association), which is the body that runs college sports, used the label I-AA between the years 1978 and 2005. Then, it started using a new name: FCS, or Football Championship Subdivision. To make the playoffs at this level, the Panthers would have to win the title of the Ohio Valley Conference (OVC), which the school joined in 1996, or get an at-large bid. EIU won the OVC in 2001 and 2002, and Tony was a major part of that story.[2]

When Tony arrived on campus, he was not the center of attention on the football team. He may have been a star at Burlington High School, but in Charleston he was just one of several hoping to play quarterback. The first time Tony's name appeared in the local paper was at the end of January 1998 when it noted that he had a 3.2 grade average, and that he was able both to sit in the pocket and to bootleg (that means to roll out to either side of the line of scrimmage) to launch passes. The story stated that Burlington went 3–6 in Romo's senior year. Lest that concern Panther fans ("Why would they go after a player from a 'bad' team"?) Coach Gerber informed locals, "We switched conferences and played some tougher competition this year." Still, Tony would have to prove himself against good players. For example, the story also mentioned that players such as Julius Davis, who was from a Chicago high school and had earned all-city honors, were in the mix. Further, there were two other candidates on campus: the backup from 1997, Jeb Odam, and a transfer, Anthony Buich.[3]

It was not certain that Romo would see much, if any, action anytime soon. As often happens with freshmen, Tony would redshirt his first year in 1998; that meant he was part of the team but did not play or use up one of his four years of eligibility (this is an NCAA rule). By the time EIU opened its season, Odam had claimed the starting position and Buich served as backup. Still, Coach Spoo had good things to say about Romo. "Tony has made great progress since he's come into camp. We do feel we have good depth even though it is inexperienced depth." After the third game of that season, Buich moved up to starter and guided the Panthers to a 5–4 record, with the team finishing the season at 6–5. He was expected to start for his senior year in 1999.[4]

While the Charleston paper provided some positive comments about Romo, his hometown reporter was more encouraging. "Former Burlington High School QB Tony Romo impressed as he went from fifth on the depth chart to second by the end of the season."[5] Mac Engel, in his 2007 book, wrote about how the freshman year was a season of adjustment for Romo, and it meant getting used to competing against better players. "In high school, Romo was the best athlete on just about every field or court he played on. College was different. . . . 'Once he figured that out, then you really started to see what this kid could do,' Spoo said." Soon, Tony did as he had in high school: he stayed after practice, worked hard, and prepared more than just about anyone else on the team.[6]

By the time the 1999 preseason started, Tony and Odam were vying for the job behind Buich, with Julius Davis listed as fourth string. This was going to be an interesting season for EIU because, for the first time, the Panthers would play three games against Division I-A teams (the highest classification)—Central Michigan, Hawaii, and Central Florida—in the same year. EIU lost their first two games against the larger schools: 33–17 against Central Michigan and 31–27 to Hawaii. The Panthers then won their conference opener 42–21 against the University of Tennessee at Martin (UTM) before losing to the University of Central Florida (UCF) Knights, 31–21.[7]

The game against UTM marked the first time Tony took the field for EIU during the regular season, and he did well. Starter Buich suffered an injured knee and Romo stepped in with the score tied at 14–14. He was ready for his chance. "Before each game I tell myself to be poised. . . . Don't be nervous. Just go play." Tony went on to complete his first four passes, including a 33-yard score. He finished the game connecting on nine of 12 attempts for 134 yards and two touchdowns. Coach Spoo was impressed: "Tony came in and ran the team beautifully. He made some good throws." His play earned him the first of the many awards he would win during his time in college: Ohio Valley Conference Newcomer of the Week Honors.[8]

Having proven himself capable of moving the offense, what would this mean going forward, especially since EIU was to play their final game against a large school, UCF in Orlando, the following week? It turned out that by Thursday of that week Spoo announced Tony as starter. Coach Wittke told the local paper that Romo had played well against UTM, but "the true test of a backup quarterback is that second week because when you get thrown into a ballgame like that you have less time to think and you just react." Still, EIU coaches were hopeful because they saw in him "a kid . . . who plays the game with a great deal of poise and can handle himself within the pocket." While UCF came into the game with a mark of 0–4, all their games were against nationally ranked teams, and they had played well. For example, just the week before, UCF lost by a score of 24–23 to the number 11 team in the country, Georgia. Tony and his teammates had their work cut out for them.[9] The result was as expected, although the Panthers only lost 31–21. Once again, Tony did well, finishing with 186 yards passing and one touchdown. His lack of experience showed early on as EIU was unable to score the first six times they had the ball. When Romo threw his touchdown pass, the Knights led 24–7 (the Panthers scored on a punt return). Still, Spoo praised his young quarterback. "He started out a little gun shy, but as he settled down, he did a pretty good job again."[10]

Romo next saw action in a mop-up role against a highly ranked OVC foe, the Tennessee State University (TSU)

Tigers. The game was close over the first three quarters, but the Tigers pulled away and were leading 36–17 when Tony came in to take Buich's place toward the end of the fourth quarter. The Panthers' starter did the best he could on his bad knee and under great pressure all day (he was sacked six times). Tony guided EIU in its final drive, hitting Andre Jones for the score, and then a two-point conversion to Nathan Kreke. That made the tally 36–25. TSU then scored again with just 27 seconds left to make the final 43–25. Although Romo led the touchdown drive of 80 yards, he got sacked three times—which meant that the Panthers gave up nine for the game.[11]

As the season progressed, two things happened: the Panthers continued to lose, and the Racine area paper continued to focus on how well Tony was doing, even during a tough season (EIU finished 2–10). The best thing, as far as Romo was concerned, was that both he and his coaches felt more assured about what the former BHS quarterback could do. "I always told my friends that Joe Montana was the best . . . because you could never get under his skin. He just went out there and played and I wanted to do that." Coach Wittke saw the same thing in the young man he helped recruit. He said that "you could see he was someone who had a knack for making plays . . . for getting the ball off and to the right people. Along with that, he showed what I thought was a presence and a poise that not a lot of people show." With starter Buich graduating, it seemed that the chance was now at hand for Tony to become the starter in 2000, which would be his sophomore (remember, he was a redshirt as a freshman) year. "We've got a good system. We run good routes. It's tough for teams to play against us."[12] Those were strong words from a young player hoping to lead a team to better results than a 2–10 record.

Before the start of the new year, two other events happened that would help shape Tony's future: first, Dan Jordan, who had played quarterback for Ohio University, decided to transfer to EIU; and second, Jeb Odam, who could have returned as a senior, decided not to use his final year. Thus, the challengers for starter were down to three: Romo, Julius Davis, and Jordan.[13]

Over the first months of 2000 the Panthers went through the routine typical for a college team's off-season: they announced new recruits, held spring practice, brought in a new defensive coordinator, held their spring scrimmage, and looked forward to a better season after their worst year in the previous twelve.[14] In regard to Tony's status, he was considered the starter, but the EIU coaches did not want to make a final decision until the beginning of the season. By early August, Romo and Davis were featured in an article that stated both were still candidates. After having to sit out in 1999 due to academic problems, Julius wanted to play: "I see it like you wouldn't be a football player if you didn't want to start." The two players had different skill sets, and Coach Spoo looked forward to using the talents of both. Not taking anything for granted, and as he had done in high school, Tony continued working to improve and over the summer of 2000, he was part of 7-on-7 drills designed to better his passing.[15] As the season approached, Coach Spoo settled on Romo as starter. While in 1999 the Panthers played against several D-I teams, the 2000 schedule featured only one such opponent: the Toledo Rockets. The second start of Tony's career came on August 31 against Indiana State University (ISU).[16]

To say he got off to a good start would be an understatement. Tony finished the game completing 13 of 14 passes for 236 yards and two touchdowns, and the Panthers won,

42–24. For this great performance, Tony once again earned OVC Player of the Week honors. The following week he did not have to do much passing since the Panthers rolled up 351 yards on the ground against a D-II school, Kentucky Wesleyan, and won, 72–0. The third week of the year brought the stern test against the larger school, Toledo. Tony played well, although he had three interceptions, with one returned for a score. Still, he threw for 414 yards and two scores, and the Panthers gave the Rockets all they could handle, but Romo's team lost 31–26. So, three games in, EIU had already matched their total number of victories from 1999. Now, they would turn their attention to foes from the OVC.[17]

Tony next guided EIU to a 42–7 victory over Tennessee–Martin. After that game (and with a week off before their next contest), Romo ranked as the most efficient quarterback in I-AA. He had completed 63.7 percent of his passes for almost 1,000 yards with nine touchdowns and four interceptions. More important, the Panthers stood at 3–1 and were ranked 27th in the country. Not bad marks for a sophomore quarterback and a team that had lost 10 games the previous year!

The following week brought homecoming and the Panthers got a scare. EIU trailed 12–0 at halftime, and 19–0 in the third quarter, against Tennessee State. Then, they roared back to outscore their foes 33–0 the rest of the way to come out on top: the final score was 33–19. Romo had one of his worst games of the year, completing only nine passes out of 27 for 106 yards and two scores. As happened with Kentucky Wesleyan, the ground game saved the Panthers, as they rushed for 273 yards. The poor performance plus some losses by the teams ahead of EIU in the top-25 poll helped move the Panthers into 25th ranking in the nation, but only in one poll. While they were gaining some attention, Tony and the Panthers still had to prove themselves.[18]

Romo followed up this game with one of his best, throwing for six scores the following week in a 48–7 rout of Murray State and tying a record set by Jeff Christiansen in 1982. Tony had 245 yards passing and four scores by halftime. Once the score got to 41–7, Coach Spoo had mercy on the Racers and EIU mostly ran the ball to keep the clock moving in the fourth quarter. This achievement moved EIU further up the polls: they came out of the game ranked 22nd in one and 24th in the other. Next came two difficult road games that would help determine the winner of the OVC: one against Tennessee Tech (TTU), and the other against Western Kentucky University (WKU). The game against TTU was close, with the Panthers trailing by a touchdown, 10–3 at the half, but with Tony throwing for 295 yards, they came back to win, 27–16. EIU now stood at 6–1, were ranked 17th in the nation, and Romo continued to lead I-AA in passing efficiency.[19] Then, all the good energy for the Panthers came crashing down against the Hilltoppers of WKU. Not only did EIU lose, 34–12, but Tony threw three interceptions and lost a fumble. The defeat ended the Panthers' hopes to win the OVC crown. Now, if they wanted to make the playoffs, they would have to win their remaining three games to get an at-large bid.[20]

Tony and his teammates wanted to complete the turn-around from 1999 and make the I-AA playoffs. Without a conference title, they had to impress the selection committee in their final games against Southeast Missouri State (SEMO), Illinois State, and Eastern Kentucky (EKU). The contest against SEMO was a rout, with the Panthers winning 38–9 and Tony throwing for 231 yards and two scores.

The game against ISU was, many thought, the final blow to the Panthers' playoff hopes, as the Redbirds won a thriller, 44–41 in double overtime. Tony had three scores, although he completed only 16 of 36 passes, and dropped to second in the nation in passing efficiency. Thus, EIU had one chance left: Eastern Kentucky University. The Panthers made short work of the Colonels, winning 49–6. Romo not only passed for 249 yards on just nine completions but also ran 62 yards for another touchdown. One of the passes (to Will Bumphus) went for 96 yards—a school record. EIU's reward was an invitation to the playoffs and a trip to play the University of Montana Grizzlies in Missoula, a major power year in and year out. Indeed, going into this game, Montana was the number one ranked team in I-AA.[21]

At halftime of the game in Big Sky Country, the Panthers trailed only 17–7. Even more hopeful for EIU, the Grizzles lost their starting quarterback at the end of the second quarter. Next, the Panthers were going to get the second half kickoff. Tony thought that if EIU could score, then it would be a whole new ball game. There was hope that this wonderful season could continue, right? It did not turn out that way. The first drive of the third quarter was a three and out. Then, Montana started to run the ball, unlike what they did in the first half. In their first drive, the Grizzlies threw only one pass and marched down the field for a score. Montana's running game caught Coach Spoo by surprise; he later said, "That really threw us off." The final score was not close: 45–13. This knocked the Panthers out of the playoffs, and they finished 8–4 for 2000. Tony summed up the year this way: "We feel good about the season. It's just really hard to take right now. We haven't been in this position all year. Western Kentucky maybe, but not like this."[22]

While the Panthers did not reach their goal of a national title, the year was certainly a success. Coach Spoo led a six-win improvement from 1999 and finished second in the voting for the Coach of the Year Award—named in honor of Grambling legend coach Eddie Robinson. Tony and cornerback Kourtney Young also gained notice and were named I-AA Honorable Mention All-Americans. Lastly, Romo claimed the OVC Offensive Player of the year. He finished with 27 scores and 2,583 yards passing. On a national level, he finished second in passing efficiency. Now, after completing his first full year as a starter, Tony and his teammates looked forward to even more success. While 2000 was a year where they made the playoffs, EIU hoped to achieve even greater things in 2001.[23]

THE BIG CAT GETS NOTICED, 2001-2002

Although it ended in disappointment, the Panthers' 2000 season was memorable. Not only did the team win six more games than it had in 1999, but Coach Spoo also earned national notice for these results, Tony Romo and a teammate were named Honorable Mention All-Americans, and even though the Panthers did not win the OVC crown, EIU made it to the I-AA playoffs. What could they do for an encore?

The early months of 2001 began with the usual off-season events: recruits, spring ball, and the Blue versus White scrimmage. While there had been questions coming into 2000 as to who would be under center, no such issue existed now: Tony Romo was the clear leader of the offense, and he hoped to continue his excellent play. The only issue was who would serve as the backup: Kyle Kissac or Todd Bridge. Julius Davis was still on campus, but he had been moved to receiver.[1]

There were questions, however, as to who would protect the Panthers' star signal caller. Three starting linemen from 2000 had graduated, and Coach Spoo needed to find replacements. Two returning players, Ramiro Avina and Matt Shober, were injured going into camp. Shober had been out since the middle of 1999 with a serious back injury. When an offense relies so heavily on its quarterback, it must protect him. Hopefully, the offensive line for 2001 would be up to the job of keeping Tony upright.[2]

While Romo should have been pleased with achieving the OVC Offensive Player of the Year Award and nearly catching Sean Payton for the most touchdowns ever thrown by a Panther quarterback in a season, with 27 (Payton had 28 in 1984—keep his name in mind, as Payton played a big part in Romo's NFL career)—he continued to work at his game. An article in the local paper in August 2001 provides an important glimpse into Tony's work ethic. One cannot help but believe that this element of Tony's character was influenced by watching, and hearing stories from, his hard-working immigrant grandfather.

The thoughts about improving his game started during the playoff loss to the Grizzlies. During that contest Romo observed a problem with how he was gripping the football and not getting enough zip on his passes. "I really noticed it on my own. I've always heard the lesson that you learn from your losses. Against Montana I knew something was wrong." This meant that Tony worked on his grip and motion throughout the whole off-season. In addition, he worked to improve his speed and strength. By the end of the summer, he showed great improvement in both areas. As to his throwing, he said that it was "rough in the spring because I changed my grip. . . . Now I'm a lot better. My velocity is a lot better. I can throw 8 to 10 yards further." Regarding the other part of his work during the off-season, he stated, "I've improved my vertical and my squat. I'm a lot quicker than I was. This year, I'm a little more mobile. I'll be able to run and throw." Here, for the first time, we also hear Tony express hope about playing at the next level. "Romo has some thoughts of a pro football career, one of the reasons he knew after watching tapes of John Elway and others he needed to alter his throwing style."[3]

The EIU coaches noticed Tony's improvement and were certainly glad that they had taken the chance to offer a partial scholarship to the kid from Burlington. Coach Spoo was hard on himself for almost passing on him. "You talk about surprises in recruiting. We were looking at a couple of quarterbacks and I voted him down. I guess that shows how much I know." Coach Wittke, the hometown Racine boy, was happy to see Tony's success on the field as well as discuss what a special player he was. "His poise and his desire . . . in crucial situations, those things all came through. . . . One of his strengths was his ability to make plays."[4] All of this hard work, in addition to his great 2000 season, had Tony touted as one of 16 leading candidates for the Walter Payton Award, which is the I-AA equivalent to the Heisman Trophy, going into the season.[5]

The 2001 schedule for EIU was favorable, as they only had to play one game against a large school, San Diego State (SDSU), in the fifth game of the season. They would start their year against Indiana State, and their other non-conference games were manageable: Southern Illinois (SIU) and Florida Atlantic (FAU).

Romo got right to work versus a school against which he had much previous success: Indiana State. The year before, he was 13 of 14 passing against ISU, and in 2001 he was 16 for 16, with three scores and 240 yards. EIU won, 44–14. Not a bad way to start the season. With the terrible events of September 11, the following week's game was cancelled, and the Panthers once again took to the field on September 24. This time, they faced a more difficult challenge, playing a road game against Eastern Kentucky. Tony had a rough start, as he missed four of his first five passes and suffered an interception. Late in the fourth quarter the Colonels led, 17–14. With the clock winding down, Romo led a final drive that ended with a touchdown pass to Frank Cutolo with around four minutes left. Although his statistics were not great—13 of 23 passes, 134 yards, and two picks—he also had two scores and led the game-winning drive. The final score was 21–17. The following week, the signal caller was back in good form, and the Panthers needed it, as they played poorly but came out on top against Tennessee Tech, 44–33. In this tilt, Romo was on target on 17 of 23 throws, and passed for 211 yards and four scores. Thus, before heading out to sunny Southern California, EIU was 3–0 and they were ranked number six in the nation in the I-AA poll. Perhaps there was a chance that a strong small school could defeat an average, larger one from I-A?[6]

The results against SDSU were not what the players and coaches hoped for. The Panthers lost 40–7, as running back Larry Ned shredded EIU for 285 yards on 30 carries. The ground attack was so strong that the Aztecs did not have to punt once. EIU, on the other hand, finished with a mere 27 yards on the ground on 23 attempts. With no ground attack, Tony was under pressure most of the game. His stats were not the greatest: 15 of 26 with two interceptions and a score. After the defeat, Coach Spoo made a very significant statement, one that would figure in Romo's future goal of playing in the NFL: "That's why they're I-A and we're I-AA." In other words, the Panthers, while a strong team against other OVC clubs, did not match up against the talent of the larger school.[7] This notion often impacts players who come out of smaller programs in the eyes of scouts for NFL teams. While a player can rack up impressive numbers in the lower divisions of college football, how will he do when competing against the best of the best at the professional level? This thought would be a major consideration by teams looking at Tony for the NFL draft once he left EIU.

The next few weeks featured some great performances by EIU and their quarterback as well as a very odd game against SEMO. In the middle of a terrific wind and rainstorm the Panthers defeated the Redhawks, 12–0, without attempting a pass! The home team had 57 offensive plays and ran for a total of 313 yards. After this odd twist, Romo had several good games in a row, all of them Panther victories. Against Southern Illinois, he went 15–18 for 253 yards and three scores: EIU 49–SIU 21. Next came a game for the ages as the Panthers defeated Tennessee State, 52–49. Tony passed for 381 yards and three more scores. Against UTM, Tony had an easy evening, as EIU rolled to a 35–9 lead at the half, on the way to a 56–16 win. He only had 13 attempts for 121 yards and a score as the ground game chewed up 382 yards. With the win, the Panthers clinched at least a tie for the OVC crown. Romo followed that performance with 241 yards and a score against FAU. At this point, EIU's mark stood at 8–1 and undefeated in five conference games. The only thing standing between the Panthers and sole claim to the OVC title was the Murray State Racers. The last regular season game of 2001 was no contest, as the Panthers won, 37–6. Tony went 15 of 21 for 306 yards and three touchdowns. This meant that EIU was, once again, in the I-AA playoffs. This time around, however, as conference champs, they would host a first-round game.[8]

Going into the postseason, the Panthers ranked third in the nation in the I-AA polls. The committee that decided the pairings, however, seeded them as the fourth-best team. In late November, the NCAA released the matchups for the first round, and EIU drew seventh-ranked Northern Iowa (UNI). The game would take place on December 1 at the Panthers' stadium, O'Brien Field. The two schools played regularly when they were members of the Gateway Conference but had not met since 1996 when UNI won 21–14 in another playoff game. Both teams featured high-scoring offenses, and the fans in Charleston expected an exciting contest. That same week Tony once again earned the OVC Player of the Year Award. His results were impressive. He threw for 2,068 yards, with 21 scores and only six interceptions. His passing efficiency was the best in the country at 178.21. His numbers for yards and touchdowns were down a bit from 2000, in part because EIU had to cancel one game right after the events of 9/11 and due to the circumstances of the SEMO game. Coach Wittke summed up Romo's regular season by saying, "He is our rock. . . . His presence gives our offense—our football team—a calmness that everything will be all right. He has done what I think is the most difficult thing to do in sports: improve upon an outstanding season." Now Tony would have a chance to build on his legacy against UNI.[9]

Unfortunately, the EIU special teams had a rough game, and UNI played on a short field most of the game. The Panthers also missed an extra point. Adam Benge, a UNI back, ran for a total of 177 yards against the Panther defense. Even so, EIU outgained UNI 525 to 486. Tony had a great game, completing 22 of 34 passes for 386 yards and five scores. He did, however, have two interceptions. When it was all said and done, Coach Spoo expressed disappointment, but also praised his team for an excellent year. "It's been a glorious run. I'm very obviously proud of this football team." With Tony coming back for his senior year, plus many other holdovers, the Panthers hoped to go even deeper into the playoffs in 2002. To cap off the year, Romo and linebacker Nick Ricks earned places on the third team All-American squad.[10]

Tony Romo headed into his senior year with the goal of getting the Panthers past the first round of the I-AA play-offs, hoping to show NFL scouts that he could compete as a pro. Going into 2002, he gained much national recognition. Two magazines chose him as their preseason player of the year and, along with Nick Ricks, he was part of the first team All-American unit. EIU was ranked number four in the nation in the preseason poll. Clearly, there were many positives for the Panthers. However, they would have a difficult schedule, as they had to play road games against two I-A teams: Hawaii and Kansas State (KSU). Both games would be tough, but the contest against the KSU Wildcats would prove a huge task as they were usually ranked in the top 25 teams in the country at the higher level of play.[11]

Even with their high ranking in I-AA, it was quite likely that the Panthers would start the season 0–2 against these opponents. That is exactly what happened. EIU lost to the University of Hawaii 61–36, although they held the ball for almost 38 minutes to the Hawaii Warriors' 22 minutes. The reason for the uneven score was that Hawaii scored several times on big plays; thus, their drives did not take much time off the clock. Tony and the offense did the best they could to keep EIU close. Romo finished 30 of 53 passes for 319 yards and four scores. He did throw two interceptions. Against KSU, the Panthers lost 63–13, but were outgained only 352 to 324. As happened in the playoff game against UNI, special teams failed EIU. In fact, the score at the end of the first quarter was 15–13 in favor of the home team, but their offense had barely played a down! The Wildcats scored on a blocked punt, a two-point conversion, and a

95–yard kickoff return. From then on, KSU ground down the EIU defense, running the ball for 230 yards. Tony had to throw more often than Coach Spoo would have liked, and the numbers showed a tough afternoon: 22 of 35 passes, one touchdown, and three picks. While Romo did not have a great game, this contest would play a part in the Dallas Cowboys' signing him as a free agent in 2003.[12]

Once the games against I-A foes were out of the way, the Panthers reeled off eight straight wins against three non-conference opponents—Indiana State, Illinois State, and Florida Atlantic University—and five OVC teams. The most important victory came in week number six against the 19th-ranked Eastern Kentucky Colonels in a game that appeared to be a lost cause. With 2:21 remaining in the fourth quarter, EKU recovered a fumble on the EIU side of the field and led 24–19. More than a few fans headed for the exits of O'Brien Field. Coach Spoo even thought, "There were moments there when I was wondering what I was going to say about a loss." Tony Romo, however, did not feel the same: "To be honest, we kind of have an aura around here now that we'll find a way to win." So, with the Panthers taking the ball with 43 seconds left, and 75 yards away from the EKU goal line, with no time-outs, the EIU signal caller led a frantic drive to victory. First, he completed passes of 12 and 10 yards. Then, an incompletion. Next came a 46-yard toss to Alfred Osborne that got the Panthers to the Colonels' 8-yard line with only 20 seconds left. After two hurried incompletions, EKU was penalized for interference, which put the ball on the 3. Right afterwards, a penalty against EIU moved the ball back to the 8. One more incompletion left only 2.4 seconds on the clock. It was do-or-die time! Tony took the snap and looked for an open receiver; seeing none, he ran the final eight yards for the score. EIU had pulled off the win, 25–24. In addition to scoring the winning touchdown, Romo threw for 359 yards and two scores.[13]

A few days after this game there was an interesting article on Tony in a major paper: *The Chicago Tribune*. Here, Romo spoke about his love of the game and interest in playing at the next level. Still, the reporter noted how big of a jump it would be to go from a small school to the NFL. "It's a huge leap from I-AA to the NFL, yet people close to Romo believe he has the arm, the poise, the work ethic, the coaching and the passion for the game to make it possible to reach what he calls 'the next level.'" The article also quoted Sean Payton (remember him?), the former EIU quarterback whose records Tony chased in his final year. As Romo finished his senior year, Payton was the offensive coordinator for the New York Giants. He would move on to be the quarterbacks' coach with the Dallas Cowboys the next season. This *Tribune* article noted that Payton "is aware of Romo and will turn his attention to him after the NFL regular season and playoffs." Thus, one former Panther was keeping an eye on a current player from his old school. Once Payton moved to Dallas, he would play a role like that of Coach Wittke and bring Romo to the attention of the Cowboys.[14]

By the middle of November, EIU had, once again, clinched the OVC with a 55–43 win over UTM, the 100th win in Coach Spoo's career at the school. Tony did his part, connecting on 17 of 21 passes for 211 yards and two scores. These touchdowns increased his season total to 28, tying him with Sean Payton's mark from 1984.[15] Tony would go on to break Payton's record the following week against FAU in a 47–6 triumph with two more scores. He then added two more in the final game of the regular season, a tough

loss on a last-second field goal to Murray State, 37–35. This defeat left the Panthers with an 8–3 mark, and although they were OVC champs, they dropped in the polls and had to play their first-round playoff game on the road. Their foes would be the Western Illinois (WIU) Leathernecks, a team coming in with a mark of 10–1.[16]

Before heading to Macomb, Illinois, to play WIU, Tony picked up some more hardware from the OVC. He was, for the third straight year, named the conference's most valuable player. He certainly merited the honor. He completed the regular season with a total of 2,950 yards passing, 33 touchdowns, and was fourth in the nation in passing efficiency. In addition, he was one of the 16 finalists for the Walter Payton Award. Now, if he could only guide the Panthers to a victory in their playoff game.[17]

Unfortunately, the contest against WIU was the last of Tony's career for the Panthers. The Leathernecks crushed EIU, 48–9, and Romo was under constant pressure during the entire game. While watching game film, the WIU coaches noticed that most of the OVC teams would use only three linemen to rush Tony, while they would drop eight players to defend against the pass. The Leathernecks took a different approach; they did not drop as many defenders into coverage, and instead applied more pressure against the EIU pocket. The scheme worked perfectly. Tony was sacked three times, was under pressure on many plays, lost a fumble, and had one interception. After the game Romo said, "That's about as much pressure as I've felt." WIU also stopped the Panthers' run game, allowing only 56 yards on 28 attempts. Although Romo did throw a touchdown pass, it was too little, too late, as the score came with WIU ahead, 34–2. It was a total team failure. Coach Spoo summed up the game by saying that "every phase of the game was below par, every phase." With his 215 yards passing this day, and one more score, Tony finished his senior year with a total of 3,165 yards, 34 scores, completed 258 of 407 passes, and 16 interceptions. Overall, he finished his time in Charleston with the following numbers: total offense, 8,059 yards; passing efficiency, 157.2; and touchdown passes, 85. Several of these marks placed Tony alongside Sean Payton. Some of these marks would be surpassed by a later Panther quarterback, who also made a mark in the NFL, Jimmy Garoppolo.[18] For the third year in a row, EIU finished 8–4, and lost in the first round of the playoffs. While this mark was a great feat in 2000, the Panthers had hoped for much, much more in 2001 and 2002.[19]

While EIU did not achieve Tony's goal to win a title, he was still in the running for an individual award, as the Walter Payton candidates were reduced to only three players in early December. His competitors for this prize were also quarterbacks: Bruce Eugene from Grambling State and Brett Gordon from Villanova. The announcement came shortly after the loss to WIU. "It's been kind of a downer the last three days. It's been kind of tough losing like that, and this gets me back into a football mode a little more." In addition to waiting for the results of the Payton voting, Tony was in line to be part of some All-Star games. Lastly, he was also going to head to Florida to work out for two weeks to prepare for the upcoming NFL draft. Coach Wittke summed up Tony's career at EIU by saying that "he's come a long way from a skinny kid from Burlington to a Payton finalist. It's a tremendous honor and well-deserved."[20]

Over the next two weeks, Tony, the rest of the Romos, and his EIU family waited anxiously for the notice of the winner, and several of them headed to Chattanooga for the announcement. Tony was relaxed about the event and the hoopla. "The only thing that would make me nervous would be making a speech. It's just an honor to be invited." The article on the lead-up to the big day also noted that NFL scouts were going to measure Tony's arm strength and other skills. Coming from a I-AA school, the local reporter hoped, they would also measure his "heart and ability to make a winning play." Coach Spoo chimed in with his hopes, saying that he believed that "his best days are ahead of him. There's a lot out there for him to accomplish." Prophetic words indeed.[21] The news that Tony had earned the Payton Award came the very next day. After hugging his parents, he then gave the speech he had dreaded. Just like leading a fourth quarter, game-winning drive, however, he pulled it off. "You know, I actually did pretty good. I kind of winged it. For some reason, it came out nice." Now that he had accomplished all that he could at the I-AA level, it was time to look toward the possibility of playing in the NFL.[22] With all this happening at the end of 2002, what could 2003 bring to Tony's life and football future?

CHAPTER 5

PROVING HIMSELF ALL OVER AGAIN, 2003–2005

Tony Romo certainly put up some great numbers during his years at the control of the Panthers' offense. In total he started 35 games, threw 941 passes, completed 584 (a 62.1 rate), passed for 8,212 yards, made 85 scores, and had an efficiency rate of 157.5.[1] Still, there were many doubts as to whether he could play at the next level. Sure, he had done well, but he was playing mostly against teams from the OVC. How would he do against players who came from D-I and played at places like Michigan? In order to get a chance to play in the NFL Tony would have to prove himself all over again. This was a much bigger stage than when he had to show Coach Spoo what he could do in order to get an athletic scholarship.

Shortly after EIU lost to Western Illinois in the playoffs and Tony collected the Walter Payton Award, he was off to Florida to participate in a camp sponsored by a group of sports agents, the International Management Group. At camp there were players from large schools such as Notre Dame, Florida State, and Oregon. It was a bit odd to see someone from Eastern Illinois there. Sure, he was the only I-AA player in camp, and sure, one of the other quarterbacks at the camp was Byron Leftwich, whom many believed would be a high choice in the 2003 draft. Still, Tony was not awed. "It's exciting. . . . I feel my talent is good enough to be here. I've had a good week of practice." Romo went to this camp, in part, to get ready for the NFL Combine, which would take place in Indianapolis on February 18–25.[2] Before heading off to Indiana, Tony played in an all-star game in Utah: the Paradise Bowl. There would be several pro scouts at this game. He did well, with two scoring passes—one for 76 yards—and believed that this game would make it possible for him to be drafted by an NFL team. "They really like my arm strength and release. . . . From talking to people, I think if the draft were tomorrow, I'd go anywhere from the third to fifth round."[3]

Next came the NFL Combine and again, Tony did well. Among the teams that approached him were Miami, Tampa Bay, San Diego, and Buffalo. One of the most important contacts was with Dallas. Romo recalled, "A coach from Dallas said, 'You really impressed us. I'm not just saying that. You really impressed us.'" Still, there were concerns. For example, he ran the 40-yard dash in 4.9 seconds. Now, that might be good for most of us, but not for the NFL— even for quarterbacks. However, his arm strength was quite impressive. By the end of the combine, Tony's passes were clocked at 57 miles per hour. The fastest throws in the NFL at the time were at around 61 miles per hour thrown by Brett Favre. "If we get close to him, we're fine." Also, Tony scored 15 points higher than any other quarterback in the combine in an IQ test, administered mostly to see how he reacted to pressure and difficult situations.[4]

While he waited for draft day in late April, Tony returned to a hero's welcome in Burlington. He was the guest of Coaches Gerber and Berkholtz and was cheered by the hometown folks at halftime of the Demons' regional semi-final basketball game. He surely drew the loudest cheers when he remarked, "Maybe I'll be in a Packer uniform this year."[5] The local reporter got reactions from scouts about Tony's performance at the combine: many were impressed by his attitude and willingness to work hard. One scout said, "Everyone's out for themselves now. There's an attitude of, 'Well, I would, but it may hurt me.' He wasn't like that at all." Here, it is not hard to glimpse the behavior of his grandparents and parents shining through and making a good impression with scouts. Tony summed up his hopes for the draft by saying, "My mindset going into the draft is that I'm going to be happy, and my family is going to be happy wherever I get drafted."[6]

While many in Wisconsin and Illinois were hoping Tony would get the call, the reality was that the odds were not in his favor. A quick look at his file by NFL scouts noted both positives and negatives. For example, they believed he was "very effective at reading defenses . . . able to go through progressions . . . shows good poise and is a vocal leader . . . [a] quick thinker who communicates well with his teammates and coaches." On the other hand, the report also pointed out he "lacks ideal foot speed . . . forces his vertical tosses and . . . needs to show better arm strength on his long balls . . . stands flat-footed at times, resulting in throwing off balance, causing the ball to sail."[7]

With the draft starting on April 26, Tony's hometown paper did a story a couple of days before the event. Here, Peter Jackel reached out to another son of Burlington, former BHS quarterback and then–running back coach for the Minnesota Vikings, Dean Dalton, to talk about Romo's draft status. Another part of Dalton's job was to scout offensive players for his team. So, what was his impression of the younger BHS Demon? "He has excellent athletic ability, excellent leadership skills and is a very bright young man." Still, there was caution as Dalton also stated that "people are all over the board on him . . . he's a great competitor and a great leader. And those are two intangibles you have to have at that position." While he must have been nervous, Tony kept up a brave front. "I didn't realize it, but a lot of teams started to gain interest during the last few months." Romo also told Jackel that there was no doubt in his mind he would be a starter in the NFL someday. "I didn't get to where I am today not thinking that way."[8]

It is always difficult for NFL hopefuls as the rounds go by and they do not hear their name called. That is how things turned out for Tony Romo on April 27 as seven rounds passed, and no one picked him among the total of 262 selections. Shortly thereafter, though, he took a call from Cowboys' owner Jerry Jones, who quickly passed the phone to his new head coach, Bill Parcells. The well-known, gruff coach had just taken the reins in Dallas after previous stops with the New York Giants, the New England Patriots, and the New York Jets. With Parcells doing most of the talking, Tony decided to sign as a free agent. "It was Parcells who sold me at the very end. He had some good stuff to say and made me feel that I really had a great opportunity there." Romo would be competing with Chad Hutchinson, Quincy Carter, and Clint Stoerner to play under center for Dallas. Parcells felt Tony could move up the depth chart. "And then he said, 'We want you to compete for the No. 2 spot . . . we do not have a starting quarterback right now. If you come in and play well . . . you have a great chance of starting for the Dallas Cowboys.'" While Tony grew up in Wisconsin, his grandparents spent much time in Texas, and they now lived there. What could be better than the chance to play for this legendary team from the Lone Star State? One has to realize that the Cowboys are not just "any" NFL team. They are one of the most elite clubs in all of American (and indeed, the world of) professional sports. Their owner, Jerry Jones—about whom you will hear a lot later—is one of the most colorful personalities in sport. In other words, Tony was stepping into a situation in which, should he succeed, the bright lights of fame would certainly be upon him. Another reason for Tony to sign with the Cowboys was that Dallas's new quarterback coach was someone already familiar with him, former EIU Panther, Sean Payton.[9]

As NFL teams started minicamps in May, Parcells believed that the starting job was up for grabs. Hutchinson had been the starter at the end of 2002, but he understood that did not mean much. Carter also felt he had a chance to earn the job going into the 2003 season. After all, both players started games for a team that finished 5–11 and they had similar results: around 1,500 yards passing and marks of seven scores and eight interceptions.[10] Those were certainly not first-rate numbers. Parcells simply said that he would look for "the guy who can get the ball in the end zone." All this uncertainty made it seem that Tony would at least get a chance to prove what he could do.[11]

It did not take long for Romo's hometown paper to start singing the praises of his showing at camp. "Under the notoriously exacting eye of . . . Parcells, Romo more than held his own during the extensive repetitions he was given." Peter Jackel also quoted Gil Brandt, another Cowboy legend, who had positive things to say about Tony. "I think he has a good chance of being probably the inactive type of quarterback or third. . . . He looked pretty accurate and that's where it starts right there."[12] As the team started a second minicamp in late May (which would last through June 7), Tony felt that he could stick with the club. Parcells "wants kids who will fight for every inch. . . . They are giving me a lot of time, and that is all you can ask for. Hopefully, if I play well, I'll stick around." He did have his ups and downs, as one day he fumbled a snap and Parcells got on him. Then, just after, Tony threw a 60-yard touchdown pass. Parcells was very happy with that result! "That's how you come back from that, Tony."

While Romo was still in the mix, he had not yet earned an important sign: a star on his helmet. He did get some upbeat words from Jerry Jones and Gil Brandt, however. Even his surly coach had some positives: "He's heady. His arm is OK." The NFL folks noted, though, how long a shot Tony was. Brandt put it this way: "Going from the Big Ten is like going from second grade to MIT. I imagine that going from Eastern Illinois to the NFL is like going from kindergarten to MIT."[13] To give you a sense of how big of a jump this is, it might be a good idea for you to read up on the story of undrafted free agents in NFL history. Among the greatest names in this group are players such as Donnie Shell, Adam Vinatieri, and James Harrison. Shell is in the NFL Hall of Fame, and Vinatieri and Harrison might be. These men, as would Tony, beat the odds. While some of these players came from large schools, the players mentioned here came from schools similar to EIU: South Carolina State, South Dakota State, and Kent State. Just like the EIU Panthers, these were not exactly major programs.[14]

With training camp in San Antonio starting on July 25, Tony was back in a city of great significance to his grandparents. After all, this was the place where Ramiro Sr. first arrived in the United States and where the Romos had owned restaurants. Perhaps this town would also be the place where the Romo family's improbable journey from hardworking immigrants to the heights of an NFL career might be fulfilled. As camp moved along Tony got more attention. By early August, reporters from Wisconsin and Illinois stated that some websites claimed that he was up to third in the depth chart. The rookie, however, knew he had not earned anything. "If I throw a couple of picks in the next two days, I'll be right back to where I was. . . . I'm trying not to be a guy who can do well one day and not the next." Indeed, Romo heard from Parcells that he would get quite a few plays against the Arizona Cardinals in the first preseason game of the year.[15]

It was in this contest that Tony was made aware of his shaky status. Rookies are expected to make mistakes, and Romo made a big one. While he had a good debut (he completed four of eight passes for 51 yards), it was an ill-advised effort that got him in trouble. Late in the game, the Cowboys were down to the Arizona 10-yard line, and Tony, under pressure, tried a shovel pass that hit an official and was intercepted. Dallas lost 13–0 and the turnover ended their best scoring chance of the game. Not surprisingly, the Cowboys' head coach was not too happy. "Parcells demands fundamental, mistake-free football and nothing triggers his quick temper more than when his team falls short of those expectations." All of this meant that Tony got a serious talking-to. "He let me have it and for good reason. It was a big moment in the game. . . . I should have been smarter with it." Still, Romo took his medicine and gained knowledge from the situation. From his first action against another NFL team, he felt that the game was "a lot faster . . . but if you can play faster and quicker, then you can play at this level. I definitely think that I can play in the NFL." He improved his second time out (although he lost a fumble), completing four of six passes for 74 yards, including a 60-yard touchdown strike against the Houston Texans. Even with his one mistake, a team reporter noted that "Parcells and his staff have been greatly impressed with Romo's poise and command of the playbook during practices and are intrigued with his potential." Just as he had done back at BHS and EIU, Romo's ability to "see" the field and understand where to go with his passes made him stand out. It seems that the IQ test he took back in Indianapolis was right about Tony's intelligence and ability to think clearly under pressure. By the time the regular season started in early September, Tony had beaten out Stoerner for the third position in the Cowboys' depth chart. During the preseason, he completed nine of 17 passes for 134 yards with one score and one interception. Yes, he was a backup, but he had made the team.[16]

The 2003 season passed quietly for Tony Romo. He watched and learned but did not see action during the regular season. The magic that Jerry Jones hoped for by hiring Coach Parcells happened, and a team that had finished 5–11 the year before went 10–6 and made the playoffs as a wild card. In early January 2004, the Cowboys' year came to an end when they lost to the Carolina Panthers, 29–10. While the result was upsetting, it had been a great year. Quincy Carter had a good season, throwing for 3,302 yards and 17 scores. He did, however, have 21 interceptions, which certainly would have bothered Parcells.[17]

One of the few times that Tony made headlines in 2003 was when the paper that covered his career at EIU reached out to him in October of that year. Tony summed up some of what had occurred in his life up to that point of the season. He stated that he was constantly told by Parcells that backups are "one play away, so stay ready." Romo also indicated that he was learning from the Dallas starter. "It's good for me to see the professionalism that he has. That's what I take from Quincy, his professionalism." He also shared that one of the jobs of the third quarterback had now changed due to technology. "I'm actually pretty lucky; I don't hold any clipboards. We have the microphones in the helmets, so I hear all the calls. I try to take mental reps every game." While he would not see any game action, Tony still believed his chance would come. "I hate to say it's like a redshirt year—but I'm learning. At the same time, I'm waiting for my time. I'm playing it like I could play every week."[18]

In a story two weeks after, Tony caught up with Peter Jackel from his hometown paper. While this article covered much the same material as the one from October, Tony did discuss some other aspects of his life. The story stated that he was making $250,000 for the year, and that his pay would increase to $380,000 for his second season. Romo noted that his one big indulgence was buying a Chevy Tahoe for $36,000. His only other regular expense was the $500 he paid to his roommate for the apartment they shared. In regard to his career, he took a very businesslike approach. "The thing about it is that I'm a rookie and I'm just basically trying to learn and get better from week to week and compete with myself." From a personal standpoint, he also noted how his dating habits had changed since leaving EIU: "I feel I'm getting older and more mature, so now it's along the line of where I want to be around someone who I enjoy their company. . . . I want someone I want to be around all the time where you can have conversations and everything."[19] The last mention of Romo came at the end of the year when a blurb in a Fort Worth paper stated

that he impressed coaches more than did Hutchinson, and that it was expected that the Cowboys would send him to play with an NFL Europe team during the off-season. Ultimately, the team decided not to send him overseas.[20]

One other aspect of the 2003 season mirrored Tony's previous experiences. When he was confronted with mechanical problems with his performance, he did everything he could to improve. Both Payton and another coach, David Lee, noticed Romo and sought to work with him. Lee, in particular, told his young player that he would have to change the way he threw the ball. It would take quite a bit of effort and time. "This is going to take a year. . . . That's muscle memory. You can't change that. It takes about 10,000 throws." Tony's response was one that would have made his grandparents and parents proud: "Let's do it now." So, off the coach and player went to change everything about Romo's motion.[21]

Going into training camp in 2004 there was talk that Romo would be sent to the practice squad. That is a group of players who attend practice but do not suit up for games. Tony would have none of this talk. If the Cowboys did not want him on the field, then perhaps another NFL team would. He went into camp believing he had improved, although nothing was certain. "The bottom line is I have to take care of business when it counts. I can't lay an egg." While Dallas did cut Hutchinson, they also brought in two new players to compete for the position: Vinny Testaverde and former Michigan signal caller Drew Henson (who had been playing baseball in the New York Yankees' system). So, the depth chart in late July looked like this: Carter, the returning starter; Testaverde, the veteran; Henson, the player returning to football after having played at the highest levels in college; and Romo, the second-year player who toiled at little EIU. Who would stick this time around?[22]

Sometimes, unexpected things have to happen for a player to get a shot to make it in the NFL. Less than one week after Romo was being considered as a possible practice squad player, a decision by the Cowboys changed his situation. On August 5, the team cut its 2003 starter, Quincy Carter. At first it was a shock, and the team was vague as to what had happened and why. The rumors were that Carter had failed a drug test. Eventually, that fact was confirmed. The main beneficiary of this was Romo, as now there were only three quarterbacks in camp. For the Cowboys, on the other hand, now only three players remained: 40-year-old Testaverde and two youngsters, Henson and Romo. In an exhibition game against Houston all three had struggled; Tony in particular had two interceptions and a fumble. Parcells wanted to give him a bit more time but was not quiet about looking elsewhere, if necessary. "Circumstances could change here as training camp goes on. . . . Right now, it hasn't happened. There is nobody out there I am interested in." So, given all of this, Romo still had a chance, but he had to do better.[23]

Dallas's second game of that preseason was one in which Tony shined but also had a bit of luck. The Cowboys won over the Raiders 21–20, and Romo led the winning drive, taking the team 59 yards on 17 plays and diving into the end zone for the final score. During this drive, he completed five of 10 passes for 40 yards, but was blessed when he had an interception called off because of a penalty against Oakland. Still, the local papers did indicate that his performance was good enough that he "might have just scrambled himself back into the quarterback mix."[24]

After this game, only two more remained in the preseason: against the Tennessee Titans and the Kansas City

Chiefs. These two games were both wins, 20–17 and 24–20. Against Kansas City, Tony had a great game: he finished 12 of 14 for 141 yards and one score. His main rival, Henson, had four attempts and did not complete a pass. This was a huge improvement over how he had done in the first three games: 12 of 25 for 109 yards and no scores. The day after this game, the papers noted that the head coach went up to Romo after he led the team on a 10-play, 70-yard drive— and finished off with a 15-yard scoring strike—saying simply, "Well done, son. You did good." Coming from Parcells, known as one of the most demanding coaches in the sport, that was high praise indeed. Once the season started, Tony got another job: as the holder for field goals and extra-point attempts. Later, Parcells commented that he was okay with Romo as Testaverde's backup, given that "he seems to be on top of things mentally, giving his coach the right answers to daily quizzes."[25] By the time October rolled around, it seemed that Tony was the backup, but Henson was being given a chance to get back to playing football after being away from the game for four years. Parcells, as always, was concerned when Romo did not do as well as he hoped in practice. "I was telling him I bet his girlfriend didn't get any teddy bears when he took her to the arcade, because he couldn't hit anything for a couple of plays."[26]

The back and forth concerning the quarterback situation continued for the whole season: the veteran started 15 of 16 games and Henson started the other. Henson's chance came on Thanksgiving Day when the Cowboys played the Chicago Bears. Things did not go well, and he completed only four of 12 passes for 31 yards with one pick. Dallas came out on top, but it was Testaverde who led the team to two second-half scores to seal the 21–7 victory. Henson did not see the field again. The Cowboys, after making the playoffs in 2003, finished 6–10. While Parcells hoped to rely on a veteran signal caller to lead his team, Testaverde's results were similar to those of Quincy Carter the year before: about 3,500 yards, 17 scores, and 20 interceptions. Tony Romo never threw a pass in the 2004 season. Clearly, things were still up in the air going into 2005.[27]

One person who was certainly not a fan of Tony's was Gil LeBreton, a local sportswriter. In an article in mid-December 2004, he made his position quite clear: "Tony Romo can carry a clipboard. Can he carry the Cowboys? The answer here is a resounding yawn." Part of the problem was that Parcells seemed to be unclear as to who was the No. 2 quarterback. Henson did not do well in the only action of the season, and Tony had not had a chance to play in a regular season game, other than as a holder. The Cowboys had spent $3.5 million on Henson and a lot less on Romo, so it seemed that they had to give Drew more time and chances. Going into the off-season, the questions about the young quarterbacks were many. Still, the head coach thought they could do the job. "I've seen something in both of them; otherwise, they wouldn't be here. . . . There's a very good chance one of those two could be the quarterback in 2005."[28]

There were also questions as to whether Testaverde would return to Dallas (he did not), so that made things even more doubtful. In the meantime, once again, the team thought about sending both Romo and Henson to NFL Europe. It would take a bit more time, but by the middle of January 2005, the situation had become clearer: eventually, Vinny returned to New York to rejoin the Jets; Jerry Jones said that Dallas would seek another experienced free agent quarterback; and the two youngsters would not go overseas but instead work closely with Sean Payton and offensive coordinator Maurice Carthon. In late February, the team signed Drew Bledsoe, who had previously been the starter with New England (until he lost his job to Tom Brady) and then went on to spend two years with the Buffalo Bills.[29]

Shortly after signing Bledsoe, the Cowboys offered Tony a contract extension. The deal was for the same amount he earned in 2004: $380,000. By the middle of March, Romo was the only team free agent who had not signed. It certainly seems that he believed in himself and what he could do for the Cowboys, and Tony wanted the team to pay him more money. While it took a couple more months, the team finally met his price. In late May, the former EIU Panther signed a deal that would pay him the amount noted above in 2005 plus a $300,000 signing bonus and another $20,000 when he reported to camp. His salary would jump to $900,000 in 2006. If he stayed with the team, and reported to camp in 2006, he would earn another $280,000, making his 2006 worth up to $1.18 million. While still not up to what his competitor Henson made, this was a substantial improvement in Tony's pay. One can only imagine the reaction of his parents—and even more so, his immigrant grandfather—when looking at these numbers.[30] Now that Jerry Jones had invested more money in his young quarterback, would Tony finally get a chance to throw a pass in the regular season?

The short answer to this last question was "no." Once again, Romo did not take the field in the regular season other than to hold, and Bledsoe guided the team to a 9–7 finish. The Cowboys, once again, did not make the playoffs, but they certainly did better than they had in 2004. The new free agent asset did well, completing over 60 percent of his passes for more than 3,600 yards, and throwing for 23 scores and only 17 picks.[31]

The newspaper reports from the Cowboys' camp and during the regular season mirrored what went on the year before. With a steady veteran at the controls, the team improved, but the young guns' only chances to shine were during practice. Once again, there were questions as to what might happen if the veteran went down. Who would come out on top for the backup slot: Romo or Henson? Going into the first preseason game (against Arizona), Parcells was, as usual, guarded. "I think I've got to see what I've got here. I told you what I've got to do, give them plenty of reps and see how it will play out in the preseason. And when that is done, if something needs to be done, we'll do it."[32]

While this back and forth continued, it is possible to discern some changes in the reporting. Even though Dallas lost to the Cardinals, some very positive comments appeared concerning Tony's play. "Romo looked poised. He flung the ball around pretty good. And while Romo might not be as add-water-and-go as some . . . he has an upside which they do not, and he proved Saturday that he can play." Just a few days later, writer Randy Galloway went even further in heaping praise. He argued that Romo had clearly earned the backup spot and quoted former Cowboy quarterback and team radio voice, Babe Laufenberg, in the process. In his view, "there wasn't even a competition. Romo has been so much better from Day One of training camp. Bill doesn't have a tough decision. It's clear-cut." New quarterback coach David Lee (Sean Payton was now the assistant head coach and would be the head coach of the New Orleans Saints in 2006) seconded Laufenberg by saying, "There's no doubt in my mind that if anything happened to Drew [Bledsoe], Tony could come in, play well, and help us win." Further, Lee went on to say that things (seeing the field and playing well) started to click for Tony in the 2005 minicamps. "And a big part of that is having a short memory. He can make a mistake, you can yell at him, chew him out, he listens, learns, and goes back into the huddle ready to go, still full of confidence. I happen to think that Tony has a heck of a future." Lastly, and even more telling, at least among the reporters at camp, "Romo has been sharper, and better, than even Bledsoe." So, by a few weeks before the start of the 2005 regular season, Romo had set himself up as the clear No. 2, and some were even wondering if he might pass the veteran free agent.[33] Quite a step up, but Romo still did not have a chance to throw a pass in the regular season.

In the meantime, Henson struggled, and toward the end of preseason did not play in a game against the Texans; that was the head coach's decision. Knowing how much they had invested in him, owner Jerry Jones held out hope that Drew would be able to return to the way he played with Michigan. Henson spoke with confidence when asked if he still considered himself the backup to Bledsoe. "'I'm really just worried about myself right now.' Henson says that he feels like he is still on pace to be the quarterback of this team one day, and Jones apparently agrees." At this point, with around two weeks to go before the start of the 2005 season, Parcells, as usual, kept his thoughts to himself. "I think I'm going to leave it up in the air until we get everything set."[34] Still, even to a former critic such as Gil LeBreton, it was clear that Tony had moved past Henson and might be able to start. "I saw training camp. Yes, Romo was better. But what I'm still having a problem with is how 262 well-scouted football players were picked in the 2003 NFL draft, and none of them were named Tony Romo."[35]

Finally, one week before the start of the season, Tony heard what he had longed to hear. "Look, when something is really unproven under fire, you always have some concern, but my confidence in the player is far superior to what it was a year ago." Coming from someone like Bill Parcells, those words must have been music to Tony's ears. He was not supposed to be in this position. He did not come from a big school, nor did the Cowboys use up a draft pick on him. The team had spent a lot of money to sign someone who came from a first-tier program and was supposed to be better than him. Still, here he was—an injury away from being first in the depth chart with Dallas. Romo was not satisfied, however; he wanted to start because he had earned the job. That would not happen until the seventh game of 2006. However, it was quite a jump from EIU to the NFL. One of the Dallas papers contacted Ramiro Jr. and asked him what he thought of his son being the Cowboys' backup. "He will succeed. I have every confidence in him, and you guys will come around too." Tony echoed his father's certainty. "Yeah, my goals are a little different than the goals people have for me. And until I reach that goal in my mind, I won't stop fighting." While he could not prove himself during the regular season in 2005, his time would come soon enough.[36]

CHAPTER 6

"ROMO, GET IN THERE"

TONY FINALLY GETS HIS CHANCE, 2006

No player wants to become a starter due to an injury suffered by the person before them in the depth chart, although it often happens and is a difficult situation for those involved. If a player earns the role of starter, that is another thing, and it does make any changes in status a bit easier. As we noted earlier, Drew Bledsoe was the starter for the New England Patriots from 1993 to 2001. In fact, he signed a large contract with the team just before the start of 2001 but was hurt in the second game. His backup was Tom Brady. Bledsoe's injury was severe: a sheared blood vessel. He almost died. Brady then led the team to the playoffs. Drew did have one last hurrah, however, as he helped guide his club to a victory in the AFC conference title game against the Steelers. Then, two weeks later, Brady led the Patriots to a Super Bowl win against the Rams. The rest is NFL history: Drew never wore Patriot colors again but went to the Buffalo Bills, winding up with the Cowboys in 2005.

At the very end of his first season in Dallas, Drew let it be known that he wanted to finish his time in the NFL as a Cowboy. "This is it. I won't go to another team. I can say that with 100 percent, no-doubt-about-it certainty." His hope was to be able to lead Dallas back to the playoffs after going 9–7 the previous year. Not all who were invested in the team were convinced, however, and critics argued that Drew was too slow and not able to move around in the pocket. Bledsoe also knew that Romo was playing well in practice and might replace him at some point. Still, Drew believed he was the starter and would not be happy as a backup. "I like and respect Tony enough I certainly want to help the guy as much as I can, but I don't think I could go into the season as the backup."[1]

As the calendar turned to 2006, it was possible to find stories in the local paper that praised Romo and compared him to other quarterbacks in the league who had "come out of nowhere," especially without being drafted. Reporter Randy Galloway, not always a fan of Tony, seemed to be changing his mind (or having it changed). The scribe even mentioned that Parcells was caught on a call to the media in Seattle making some positive statements about Romo. There was also talk that Sean Payton, who now coached the Saints, wanted to bring Tony to New Orleans. Other writers, such as Jennifer Floyd Engel, continued to believe the Cowboys should stick with the veteran Bledsoe. Also, in the background (meaning NFL Europe), Dallas still held on to Drew Henson, who was playing in Germany over the spring.[2]

Heading into camp, questions remained about Tony's ability to do the job, and not all local media were on board with the idea of him as part of the Dallas Cowboys' future. Jim Reeves, for example, in early August argued that the team should have brought in another experienced backup rather than rely on the unproven Romo. "The Cowboys' hopes and dreams of a Super Bowl season rest entirely on the shoulders of their not-so-mobile quarterback. He goes down, so will the 'Boys." Considering that the team had given up many sacks in 2005, keeping Bledsoe upright was a concern. If the worst did happen, would Tony be able to win? Parcells continued to speak well of Romo and was determined to give him plenty of chances in the preseason. The first would come against the Seahawks in the Pacific Northwest.[3]

In the lead-up to this game, doubts continued about Parcells' plans for this critical position. Should not Bledsoe take at least some snaps in the opener to get him ready to go? How could the veteran coach put so much upon the shoulders of a player who had not ever thrown a pass in the regular season? Parcells stuck to his idea. "I've calculated what I'm doing here, and I think this other thing is more important right now." It seems that the coach was a bit smarter than the reporters after all. Tony led the team to a 13–3 win, hitting 19 of 25 passes for 235 yards. This was a great result, considering that on the first drive of the night a receiver dropped Romo's first pass, then a lineman moved on the second play, and finally, Tony fumbled on the next snap. Not a good start, to say the least! After the game, however, not only was the head coach happy, but so was owner Jerry Jones. "I am impressed with the way he came back and moved the team. I don't think we could have drawn it up any better, the challenges."[4]

Now, a single good game in preseason does not make one a starter, but the tide was turning. While some reporters continued their support for Bledsoe, there was a sense that a "Camp Romo" was taking shape among some in the media, as well as a good number of Cowboy fans. One player who did lose out, at least in Dallas, was the *other* Drew in the mix, Henson, as the Cowboys finally decided to move on and traded him to Minnesota in late September.[5]

By early September, Mac Engel headed an article, "Bledsoe Totters; Romo Prepares," in which he examined where things stood. In the preseason finale against the Vikings, Drew took some serious hits, reminding fans that Tony could be under center at any moment. Stepping in for the veteran, Romo had a superb game and threw for 349 yards. The game ended in a 10–10 tie, as Dallas had three turnovers in the red zone, and their kicker missed two field goals. It was an impressive performance. It is important to note here as well that the day before this game, the team signed Tony to an extension, including a $2 million signing bonus. Thus, it was not a surprise when Jerry Jones argued that the money "says a lot for Tony Romo relative to how he feels about himself and how we feel about him to get that kind of commitment." While Dallas went into the 2006 season with Drew Bledsoe as their starter, his backup was not far behind in the head coach's mind.[6]

It did not take long for fans to start grumbling. On opening day, the Cowboys played the Jaguars in Jacksonville. While Bledsoe had a good first quarter, and Dallas led 10–0, things went downhill from then on. In one specific play, Drew overthrew a wide-open Terrell Owens, which otherwise would have made the score 17–0. Between the second and third quarters, his passes gained only 42 yards. Most disappointingly, the veteran had three interceptions to only one score. The loss stirred up even more talk about Romo. One reporter argued that "Bledsoe needs a bounce back performance. . . . Parcells says he didn't consider making a move . . . against the Jaguars and will not make a change this week." Another scribe was even more gloomy: "But however long the Bledsoe leash, it just got shorter. . . .

Jerry was trying to stay positive on Bledsoe. Big Bill preferred to stay silent on Bledsoe."[7]

There is an old saying in football: "No one is as popular as a backup quarterback." This means that when a starter is not doing well, many in the grandstands and newspapers start to look longingly at the next man up to see if he can do better. That was certainly the case in Dallas. At least one local reporter still wondered just how Tony would perform. If Bledsoe did not do well against the Cowboys' next foe, Washington, he figured it was likely that Parcells would make the change. To what result? "What we get then is anybody's guess . . . former Cowboys' quarterback Babe Laufenberg has been touting Romo for several years. He loves his quick release." Sure, he might be a "gunslinger," but "I'm not sure that Romo is ready for what he's about to receive."[8]

Over the next few weeks, the Cowboys and Bledsoe had their ups and downs. After their fifth game, the team stood at a very average record of 3–2. Their veteran quarterback reflected the mediocrity. By this point, he had thrown for five scores and eight picks. His highest yardage since the first game in Florida was only 223. He also had a second contest in which he threw three interceptions.[9] For their sixth contest, Dallas hosted a longtime rival, the New York Giants, in Texas. The Cowboys lost, 36–22. This game, however, proved to be Tony's big opportunity.

October 23 was the day that Romo had been waiting for since his time at Burlington High School. The game started off with the visitors taking a 12–0 lead early in the second quarter. With New York driving again, the Dallas defense made a play and intercepted Eli Manning. Then, Bledsoe drove the Cowboys down the field 80 yards to make the score 12–7. After the kickoff, the defense again came through and handed the offense the ball on the Giants' 14. With a short field, and a chance to take the lead, Drew had another interception when Dallas was at the four-yard-line. Thus, at the half, with their veteran having thrown two more picks, Parcells informed another coach that he had made his decision to change quarterbacks. The other coach soon said to Tony the words he had yearned to hear for so long: "Romo, get in there." All those years of hard work, study, and effort were about to come to culmination: Tony would start the second half of the contest!

It did not go well right off the bat. His first pass attempt in a regular season game was intercepted and the Giants scored again, making the tally 19–7. Next possession, Romo drove the offense down to the New York 32, but a receiver dropped his pass on fourth down. The Giants then drove down the field for another touchdown, making it 26–7. Finally, in the fourth quarter, Tony threw his first NFL score, and Dallas added a two-point try to make it 26–15. Next, New York turned another interception into a field goal and the score was now 29–15. Continuing to throw on most every play, the Cowboys drove down to the Giants' four, but then another pick was returned 96 yards for a touchdown by the defender. Lastly, Tony threw a 53-yard score in the final minutes, to round out the scoring.[10] In total, he connected for 227 yards, had two touchdown passes, but suffered three picks.

Not surprisingly, Bledsoe was not happy. Neither were the fans who had long hoped for this change. Tony showed potential, but it was obvious that he needed more opportunities to learn at the NFL level. He would get his first start the next week against the Carolina Panthers.[11] Although he had gained the support of his coach, Jerry Jones was disappointed that Parcells had made the change. He saw this as a sign of desperation. After the 3–3 start with Bledsoe at the helm, "It hasn't worked out as of today. It just hasn't worked out. That to me is a step back."[12]

While the owner might have had his doubts, Tony went into the game in Charlotte with great confidence. Reporter Clarence Hill Jr. noted as much in his article prior to the game. "There is no question that Romo believes he is good enough. Credit his personality, moxie and hard work, but for an unknown player, Romo has his teammates believing he can get the job done." Heading into his first start, Tony was already taking a long-term view of things. "I don't deserve any [congratulations] until you do something in this league. There have been plenty of guys who have been . . . flash in the pans. My perspective is you need to have a career. . . . We all will find out if I am good enough." He would make a pretty good first impression on the field in North Carolina.[13]

Again, things did not start off well. Dallas missed on a field goal attempt and Carolina drove 62 yards to score, making it 7–0. Next, Tony suffered his one interception and that placed the ball on the Cowboys' 24-yard line. After a run by Steve Smith, the score now stood at 14–0 for the home team. Then, Romo hit his stride, leading the offense on 47- and 68-yard drives to cut the lead to 14–10 at the half. The third quarter did not see any big plays, as Dallas only drove down to the Panther 42, and Carolina only made it as far at the Cowboys' 37. Things broke open in the final quarter, however. Tony led a 14 play, 71-yard drive for a field goal to narrow the lead to one point. On the ensuing kickoff, Carolina fumbled, and Dallas scored on a 14-yard run by Julius Jones. Romo then flipped a pass to Terrell Owens for a two-point conversion. The score was now 21–14. The defense held off the Panthers for the rest of the contest, and Dallas scored two more touchdowns on running plays. All told, the offense racked up a hefty total of 414 yards. Final score: Dallas 35, Carolina 14. Tony finished the game going 24 of 36, for 270 yards, with one score and one interception. While it was just one game, had the Cowboys found their quarterback of the present—and the future?[14]

While the local media were happy with the results, professional football is a "what have you done for me lately" business, and soon questions started as to whether Tony's results had been a fluke. Mac Engel's column, for example, sought to lower expectations. Bill Parcells, happy though he was with the outcome against Carolina, echoed the sentiment. "There is some demonstrated ability. . . . But, you know, anyone can land a lucky punch." Jerry Jones chimed in, saying, "Everybody seems to have more confidence and play better when the future looks bright." A bit better than Parcells' review, but Engel then brought everybody back down to earth. "The future has been bright before at Valley Ranch. But every time the Cowboys looked like they have shaken the .500 virus . . . they revert back to the gang that made self-inflicted wounds into an art." Still, Tony stayed cool, calm, and collected (just as he had done at BHS and EIU) as the newfound notoriety swirled around him. Coach Parcells certainly helped in this regard. First of all, he told Tony, the next opponent, Washington, now had film and they could better prepare for the young quarterback. Second, the head coach did his best to cut off what was coming to be known as "Romomania." "Get all of your congratulatory e-mails out of the way. Now you can come and play this week maybe, huh?" Tony just laughed at that last remark. Going into his second start, he simply, and confidently, said, "I feel I can get the job done."[15]

Given the very limited sample size, it is understandable that there were still doubters. Jennifer Floyd Engel, for example, indicated in her column before the game against Washington that while Parcells certainly had a lot riding on this decision, Romo had even more so. "Because players like him [meaning an undrafted free agent from a school like EIU] do not necessarily get 101 chances . . . before NFL types finally . . . admit 'OK he really does stink.'" She then went on to state the fan base would have a "definitive answer" as to whether Tony would be the starter for the long haul after the game in our nation's capital. Parcells, direct as ever, believed he had made the right decision. "The time to worry is when you place your bet. The bet is down now. The wheel is spinning. I didn't say, 'I wish I didn't bet that.' I can't do that. You have to play the game."[16]

Tony showed that his level of play against Carolina was no fluke, as he had very similar results in his second start. Unfortunately, the Cowboys lost, though it was not because of failure on his part. Romo matched his number of throws and completions from the previous week but increased his yardage gained to 284. More importantly, he had two scores and no interceptions. Dallas lost to their rival on a freak play. With the score tied 19–19 the Cowboys attempted a field goal, which was blocked. The ball was picked up by a Washington defender who ran toward the Dallas goal line. He was tackled, but in the process the tackler grabbed a face mask, adding 15 yards to the return. Washington then kicked a field goal with no time left on the clock. Final score: Washington 22, Dallas 19. The most important result from this defeat, however, was the notion that maybe, just maybe, Romo was the answer to the Cowboys' quarterback issue. "The shame of the loss is that the formerly unproven and unknown Romo was better in his second start than in his first." After suffering his first loss as a starter, he commented, "We'll bounce back from this, but gosh darn, it's frustrating we didn't get [this] one." Although Dallas now stood at 4–4, it looked as if they might have found the quarterback of the future.[17]

Just before his third start, against a poor Arizona Cardinals team, the talk was about how quickly Tony had energized the offense and the vast improvement the Cowboys had seen in the quarterback position. For example, over the first two games, Romo completed almost 65 percent of his passes; Bledsoe had only done 53 percent. In his two starts, Tony had passed for 270 and 284 yards; Bledsoe did not top 250 in any of his outings. Most important, the young player's ability to move in the pocket—and thereby escape pressure—made it possible for him to buy time and get the ball out to various receivers. Romo even heard praises from one of his most excitable teammates: Terrell Owens. "He's a good quarterback. He's gotten us out of some wild situations making plays with his feet and obviously with his arm."[18]

The positive results continued against the Cardinals, as Tony threw for 308 yards and two more scores in a 27–10 victory. After three starts, local pundits were singing Romo's praises. One, Jim Reeves, even went back and talked with one person who had believed all along: Babe Laufenberg. In their discussion, the former Dallas field general certainly was not shy (although he says that was not the point of the interview) about saying "I told you so." All the way back to 2003, Babe thought that there was something special in the kid from EIU. "He just seemed to have that 'something.' You could never bring it back on a scouting report, but it was there. . . . This isn't happening by accident, the way he's playing." Even with so many jumping on the bandwagon,

Laufenberg reminded readers that there would be bumps along the way. "There's a bad game coming . . . and there'll be more after that if he keeps playing. But he's handled things, the reads, the blitzes, all of it . . . how well he's doing right out of the box." Given that Dallas' next game would be against the Indianapolis Colts and their great quarterback, Peyton Manning, Tony would have a chance to see just how he stacked up against someone hailed as the "best of the best" in the NFL in 2006.[19]

As if the first three starts of Tony's career were not sufficient to arouse visions of future Super Bowl wins in the minds of Cowboy fans, the victory against the undefeated Colts (they were 9–0) in game 10 of 2006 surely did. Manning had a rough outing, with two interceptions (including a pick six) and a fumble. He did throw for two scores and 254 yards. Romo, on the other hand, did not throw a touchdown (first time that happened), but managed the game with only one pick and 226 yards. The most important part of the story was that he led the offense on two fourth-quarter drives, one of 68 and the other of 80 yards, to produce two scores to put Dallas ahead, 21–14. Indianapolis then drove down to the home team's 8, but Manning missed on passes on third and fourth down. With the victory sealed, Tony took a knee to run out the clock. In an indication of great joy, he held the ball aloft for the fans as a sign of triumph while running off the field.[20]

Romo followed up this win with his best performance so far, throwing for 306 yards and five touchdowns (with no interceptions) against Tampa Bay on Thanksgiving Day, a 38–10 mauling. Now, he and the Cowboys would have more than 10 days to bask in the glow of what they had accomplished over the past month. Then, they extended their winning ways by beating the Giants in New Jersey,

23–20. Tony did not have a great game, throwing for 257 yards and two picks without a score. Still, it seemed that all was going in the right direction for the team and their young field general. They now stood at 8–4 and were favorited to win their division.

There was even a story about Tony in *Sports Illustrated*. Here, he recounted what had happened to him at a recent Dallas Mavericks basketball game. After the win against Tampa, when it was announced he was in the stands, "the crowd of 20,000 chanted his name." His reaction was simply, "It got a little crazy there. That was the first time I felt like it was really getting different." Still, as far as writer Tim Layden was concerned, "He has handled the transformation gracefully." Even teammate Jason Witten noted that Tony's goals were quite simple, just as they had been at Burlington High and Eastern Illinois: "He's not caught up in any of this. He just wants to win." On a personal level, Tony was spotted around town dating starlets such as Jessica Simpson and Carrie Underwood.[21]

Dallas's next opponent would be a team headed by a familiar face: Sean Payton, who brought his New Orleans Saints to Texas. Given all the positive events in the past weeks, now was the time to remember what Babe Laufenberg had said as "Romomania" was taking off: there would surely be less impressive outings somewhere down the line. Well, here it was! Tony and the rest of his teammates struggled, and lost, 42–17. Everything that could have gone wrong, did. Although he did have one touchdown pass, a 34-yard strike to Owens, the rest of the day was a bust. Romo finished 16 of 33 for 249 and had two interceptions. Almost immediately, doubters resurfaced. For example, one reporter noted that this had been "another subpar outing from Romo, who looked nothing like the quarterback sensation he had been in the previous six weeks." Such is the life of most NFL quarterbacks. When you do well, everyone is on board; when you have a bad game, many folks want to jump off the bandwagon. How would Tony respond?[22]

The answer came on the road the following week, as Romo's results against the Atlanta Falcons were described as being "efficient, if not spectacular." After such a poor outing, the important thing was to come out with a victory, which the Cowboys did, 38–28. With the score tied 21–21 at the half, the home team scored a touchdown at the start of the second half to take the lead. That was when Tony hit his stride. He missed only three passes in the third and fourth quarters and led Dallas to two touchdowns and one field goal. Overall, he finished 22 of 29 passes, for 278 yards and two scores. He also had one interception. Having trailed in the second half, and after being embarrassed at home the previous Sunday, it would have been easy for the Cowboys to give up. But they certainly did not. As Tony remarked after the contest, "The teams that really have a chance come January bounce right back and win. At the end, that showed a lot of character." This win moved the Cowboys into the playoffs for the first time in two years.[23] After the win in Georgia, only two games remained in the 2006 season, both of them at home: the first against Philadelphia, and the other against a very poor team from Detroit.

As a result of all the attention to Tony's rise to stardom over the past weeks, the networks wanted to get the Cowboys on television as often as possible. On Christmas Day, Dallas squared off against their longtime rivals, the Eagles. Instead of an exciting matchup, however, it turned out to be a complete dud. Philadelphia totally dominated, winning 23–7. Romo's results were the worst of his short time as a starter: 14 of 29 passes, 142 yards, two interceptions. His ability to run was the only thing that kept things from being even worse. Tony was sacked three times but was running away from pressure most of the day. Still, he was professional enough to credit his foes' efforts: "I had to throw the ball away a bunch. That's a good job by them." It appears that the Eagles showed some looks on defense that confused the young quarterback. Ramiro Jr. commented that one particular blitz was something that his son "had never seen before. . . . He never saw that guy coming. . . . He's getting the whole perspective." In a column the next day, Mac Engel pointed out that Tony had come down to earth. In November, he had thrown for nine scores and one pick; in December, the numbers were reversed, with more interceptions (seven) than touchdowns (four). Even with these concerns, however, Jerry Jones still believed in this rising star and felt that what was needed was for all the players to do their jobs correctly: "We've just got to execute." Surely it would be possible to regain confidence going into the playoffs against the Lions, who came into the last game of the year with a record of only 2–13, right?[24]

That was not how things turned out. Two local reporters wrote after the Lions left Texas Stadium with an unexpected 39–31 win that "Romo has lost his magic" and "Romo has lost his swagger." While the defeat was certainly not all his doing, he made several key errors. Tony completed 23 of 32 passes for 321 yards (his career high at this point) and tossed two scores. He also had an interception and endured four sacks.

With Dallas trailing 30–24 midway through the fourth quarter, Romo pulled out two plays that must have enraged, then greatly pleased, Coach Parcells. With the ball on the

Cowboys' 3-yard line, Tony went back to pass and, while in his end zone, dropped the ball. A Lions' recovery would have surely been the end of any hopes by Dallas. The ball bounced up to the signal caller, and he threw a 14-yard completion to Terrell Owens for a first down. Then, two plays later, the pair hooked up again for a 56-yard touchdown to pull the home team ahead, 31–30. Of course the Cowboys would pull this out! It was not to be, as Detroit went on a 72-yard drive to retake the lead, 36–31. When Dallas got the ball back, Romo fumbled (his fourth of the game), the Lions recovered and kicked a field goal. Still, the Cowboys had one more chance, as Tony led them down to their foe's 6-yard line. On fourth down, his scramble fell short at the 2-yard line, ending all hopes. "That was a symbol of Romo's past four weeks. . . . For every outstanding play he makes, there's an empty one of error soon to follow." This was certainly not the way to close out the season. Dallas failed to win their division and entered the playoffs as a wild card. As Tony noted, "It's one of those weeks where I'm going to have to let it go today when I get out of here." It seemed that the loud cheers that had greeted him previously had faded. Indeed, he even heard a few boos from the fans. Now, there were, once again, questions as to whether he could handle the job. "The Cowboys limp into the playoffs struggling in a lot of phases, including quarterback." Unfortunately, things would only get worse for him in the playoff game against Seattle.[25]

Just a few days before the game against the Seahawks, Coach Parcells noted that he believed part of what happened to Tony in December was that he had so much success in November (and so much acclaim) that he became overconfident. He was too much of a "gunslinger" and could be careless. "You guys were laughing at me when I was saying it was a little less than perfect. I think what you've witnessed is what I was talking about." Still, there were those in the media who had not jumped off the Romo bandwagon. While he deserved some of the blame, Randy Galloway argued, going into the Pacific Northwest Romo remained the best hope for Dallas to win, especially given how poorly the defense had played over the past few games.[26]

Despite the recent setbacks, Dallas went into Seattle confident of victory. While their young quarterback had struggled recently, he had had a very good year overall. Tony completed 220 of 337 passes for 2,903 yards and 19 scores. He did have 13 picks. His overall passing rating was a more than respectable 95.1. In addition, the Cowboys would play against a Seahawk defense that had endured some key injuries. While Tony did not have a great game in his first playoff appearance, he finished 17 of 29 for 189 yards and a score, and his teammates chipped in with some positive plays. Miles Austin, for example, returned a kickoff 93 yards for a score. The Cowboys' new field goal kicker, Martín Gramática, hit from 50 and 29 yards away. The defense, unlike the last few weeks, played well, limiting Seattle to only 332 yards of offense. They even stopped the home team's offense close to the goal line on fourth down. Then, things began to go wrong. At that moment Dallas led, 20–13. From his own 2-yard line, Tony audibled out of a running play and threw a short pass to Terry Glenn. The receiver made the catch, but then fumbled the ball out of the Dallas end zone, which produced a safety and two points for the Seahawks. That made the score 20–15. After the Cowboys punted the ball on a free kick, the home team drove down the field for a score. That made it 21–20 and set up an opportunity for

Tony to be the hero and drive his team down the field for a score to possibly win the game.

All looked to be going well as the offense moved from the Dallas 28 to the Seattle 2-yard line. This set up Gramática for a 19-yard field goal attempt. Even at the high school level, this short a kick is relatively easy. The team attempting to score simply needs to snap the ball and protect against a block; the holder catches the ball, places it on the ground, and the kicker knocks it through. Simple, right? Well, sadly, that is not what happened. The snap was good, but Tony, after having served as holder for many games, was not able to handle the snap cleanly, and Martín could not get the kick on its way. In a mad dash, Tony scrambled toward the Seattle goal but was stopped short. This was a shocking turn of events! Seattle took over with a little more than one minute to go, but Dallas stopped them again, and their offense had one last chance. Finally, a long pass attempt by Romo toward the end zone fell incomplete, and Seattle won, 21–20.[27]

Not surprisingly, Tony felt he cost his team the game and was heartbroken. "This will sit with me for a long time. . . . It hurts real bad to think about it." While his teammates tried to console him, when the team returned to Texas, and coaches broke down game film, one unnamed coach supposedly said, "That game may be a black mark on Tony Romo for the rest of his career. He may never get over that."[28] Of course, the naysayers returned with a vengeance. What would happen to Romo? Could he get over this? What would happen to Coach Parcells, who seemed to have lost his magic touch? The questions about the head coach ended quickly, as Parcells left Dallas and signed on to work as an executive with the Miami Dolphins.[29]

In regard to Romo's future, the jury was still out. Gil LeBreton was not negative but did express concern. "Worst of all, there appeared to be enough mistakes . . . that Romo's NFL future doesn't seem quite as paved with yellow bricks as we once thought." Randy Galloway, on the other hand, was much more positive and willing to see what the future held. "Tony Romo will be fine. If the bobble blow[s] out [his] brain cells, and destroys him, then he wasn't the guy for the job anyway." In an overview of the season, the final thoughts on Tony were these: "To a man, the Cowboys believe in Tony Romo. He will go into next season as the team's unquestioned starter. . . . Overcoming [the snap] could make him a stronger quarterback in the future."[30]

While there certainly had to be disappointment in Dallas, the rest of the league took notice of Tony's play and rewarded him by naming him as a reserve to the Pro-Bowl, the NFL's All-Star game, which in 2007 was played the week after the Super Bowl. Tony stepped in to replace Drew Brees of the Saints and performed well. He led three strong drives for the NFC, including tossing a touchdown pass of 47 yards to Steve Smith with less than two minutes to go in the fourth quarter to tie the contest. Then, the AFC drove down the field and kicked a field goal as time expired to win, 24–21. Tony threw for 156 yards and the score. While he certainly wished he could have taken his club farther in the playoffs, the 2006 season was a breakthrough for Tony Romo. He went from being an undrafted player, to backup, to the starter of one of the marquee franchises in the NFL. He still had a lot to prove given the ups and downs of the season, but he had certainly come far from a late start in his football career at Burlington High School.[31]

CHAPTER 7

ETHNIC PRIDE, BUT COMING UP SHORT ON THE FIELD, 2007-2011

Although the season ended poorly, Tony achieved a great deal in 2006 and became a subject of much interest. As a result, reporters dug further into his childhood. By late December 2006 and early January 2007 reports on this topic appeared. The fact that the new quarterback of the Dallas Cowboys was of one-half Mexican descent likely surprised many. After all, "Romo" does not obviously sound Latino; indeed, the surname could just as easily be of Italian origin.

Just before the game in Seattle, Mac Engel visited with Ramiro and Joan in their "1,100-square-foot home" in Burlington. Engel maintained that Tony's success was due not only to his abilities but "because of how and where and by whom he was raised." This story detailed the many sports Tony played, how life had changed for his parents in 2006, and the broad support Romo had in his youth both inside and outside the family. Engel stated that Ramiro and Joan raised their boy to know that he had to remain humble, no matter what. Indeed, after one poor performance in 2003, his dad told Tony that it might be best if he travelled with him, as the team might have left him in Houston and that he "might get cut." Way to keep your son in check, Ramiro! That article did not specifically mention Tony's Mexican American ancestry.[1]

In July 2020, reporter David Flores, of the *San Antonio Express-News* and local station KENS, retired after a 43-year career (he started in Kingsville in 1977). While he covered many sports during his time, he often focused on Spanish-surnamed athletes.[2] Not surprisingly, he contacted Ramiro Sr. and Feli early on in Tony's time with Dallas. In an article originally published in Texas but picked up by *The Journal Times* in Racine, Flores went in depth about the Romos' story. Here, Flores asked Tony's grandparents how they felt about their grandson becoming an NFL starter. Ramiro's mind went back in time to his first days in the United States. "I thought of how far we've come, not only as a family, but as a people. I remembered the hard times in Mexico and how I struggled when I first got here." Given the elder Ramiro's strong ties to the Catholic faith, he also mentioned that his grandson needed to keep all aspects of life in perspective. The elder Romo did this for Tony, in part, by leaving "him a scripture on his message machine before a game." Lastly, and of great importance, Granddad reminded Tony to remain true to himself and his heritage. "I told my son and my *nieto* never to try to hide their culture. . . . I'm proud to say that they've never run away from being Hispanic."[3]

It seems that the lessons he learned at the Romo household made an impact. In an interview with a *Chicago Tribune* reporter, Tony showed how modest he was by saying, "I've never been a guy who's going to use that [status] to do anything. . . . I'm from a small town, from a small college. Stuff like that just isn't warranted around those places, and I don't think I'm changing anytime soon."[4]

During the early months of 2007, the Cowboys moved on from the letdown of their playoff loss, and it was soon time to prepare for the upcoming season. By early September, as the Dallas Cowboys readied to play the Giants in the first game of the year, local scribes reminded Tony to hang on to the ball and wondered if he would be able to move past the event in Seattle. Clarence Hill certainly thought so. In his column the day before the New York game, he asserted that Romo would do well and that his play would be "enough to wake up the echoes of great Cowboys quarterbacks" in the minds of many in the fanbase. Tony's poise on the field, his hard work in camp, and the amount of time he spent watching film had made believers out of many in the locker room. In addition to having to overcome his playoff miscue, Tony had his financial future at stake. His contract with Dallas was to end after 2007, and Jerry Jones needed proof that he could depend on him before spending the millions usually paid to starting quarterbacks.[5]

It did not take long for Tony to show that he was over the dropped snap. In the game against the Giants, he threw for four touchdowns and even ran in for a score: his first in the NFL. Dallas won, 45–35. The good times continued to roll for the next few weeks, as he threw for two more scores against Miami and Chicago and accumulated over 300 yards in games against the Bears and the Rams. As the weeks passed, Tony's value to the team increased, and that meant his contract would be worth even more. Then came a night in Buffalo that Tony would prefer to forget.[6]

The Cowboys came into Western New York with a 4–0 mark. They would leave with their record intact. However, Tony had the worst game of his career. He threw five interceptions, two of which the Bills returned for scores. Still, he had two touchdown passes and led two drives for scores in the final seconds. The first was a touchdown strike that came with 20 seconds left and then, after an onside kick, Dallas kicked a game-winning field goal to triumph, 25–24. Although he had a terrible night, many were impressed by his efforts that helped, in the end, to produce victory.

Jim Reeves made this the central point of his article the day after the game. Tony, he argued, "can still pull himself together to win a game when it's there to be won." Certainly, this meant that Dallas was ready to challenge the Patriots for supremacy in the NFL, right? They would have a chance to prove that at home the following week.[7] Unfortunately for the home team, Tom Brady played very well, throwing for almost 400 yards and five touchdowns. Tony had two scores, but the Cowboys' defense could not hold down the Patriots. The final score was 48–27.[8]

After another win, this time against the Vikings, Dallas had an off week. It was during this time that Jerry Jones reached agreement with his quarterback on a new contract. The deal was for six years and $67.5 million. Surely, Ramiro Sr. could have never imagined such a bounty for someone in the Romo family! Soon thereafter, Tony showed that he was worth this large sum, as he led Dallas to a win against the hated Eagles. He completed 20 of 25 passes for 324 yards, three scores, and only one pick. The future seemed bright indeed![9]

As the calendar turned to late November, a very important game was on the horizon for this native son of Wisconsin on Thanksgiving Day, against the squad he rooted for as a boy: the Green Bay Packers. Not only was Tony playing his favorite team, but they were also led by his hero: Brett Favre. Certainly, this was a dream come true for a boy from Burlington! Tony performed well and outdid his idol, throwing for 309 yards and four scores. The

Cowboys won, 37–27. Not only that, but he also set the team record for most touchdown passes in a season (up to 33 at this point—the previous mark had been 29 by Danny White), as well as connecting for passing scores in his six-teenth consecutive game. At this point, Dallas was 11–1. They defeated Detroit the next week, and Romo threw two more touchdowns.[10]

Things changed, however, on Sunday, December 16. Against the Eagles, Tony's string of games with scoring passes ended with a thud, as he completed only 13 of 36 attempts, had three interceptions, was sacked four times, and fumbled twice. The naysayers, once again, came out in full force. Randy Galloway chimed in, stating that, "When Romo stinks it up . . . the Cowboys have zero answers. . . . It's a Romo world, both the good, and now the bad." Likewise, Jennifer Floyd Engel was not subtle in her criticism. "Decembers have long been where promising Cowboys teams fade. . . . Of course, this holiday season was supposed to be a lot jollier." Dallas was headed for the play-offs, but the concerns from earlier years were, once again, rearing their heads.[11]

Dallas split its final two games of the season, to finish off with a 13–3 record. That meant they would host a play-off game. Since they won their division, Dallas had a week off before playing. During that time, Tony took a short vacation to Mexico and brought starlet Jessica Simpson along. Some fans were not happy with this decision, given what happened in Seattle. Still, there were many in Dallas who did not see a reason to worry. After all, Tony had the best single season of any signal caller in Cowboys' history in 2007. He threw for 4,211 yards, had 36 scores and 19 picks, while completing more than 64 percent of his passes. Tony, as usual, took things in stride: "I know what I needed to get myself in a position to hopefully be successful. . . . I was able to put the phone aside and get myself ready and watch some football for two straight days." At least one local scribe, Newy Scruggs, believed that all of this would blow over when Dallas won its home playoff game. "Romo has yet to win a playoff game. . . . Time for Romo to get his first victory." The foe coming into Dallas would be a familiar one: the New York Giants.[12]

Cowboys fans all over the nation looked forward to "welcoming" the team from the big city to Texas for a second time. After all, the season started with Dallas whipping the visitors, 45–35. Then, in their ninth game of 2007, the Cowboys won against the Giants in New Jersey, 31–20. Surely, this third meeting would produce the same results, right? Well, not quite. The home team outgained the visitors by more than 100 yards (336 to 230) and controlled the ball for 13 more minutes, 36:30 to 23:30, two figures that usually mean victory. However, the Cowboys also had 11 penalties and the Giants hurried Romo in the pocket all game long. The result was a New York victory, 21–17. To say that fans, the players, and coaches were upset would be an understatement. Tony completed 18 of 36 passes for 201 yards, one score and one pick. The interception came with just nine seconds remaining in the game.[13]

Immediately, the blame for the loss fell on his shoulders. Why did he have to go to Mexico? Should he not have stayed in Texas and spent more time watching film or preparing for the game? The issue of the trip was front and center with reporters the next day. David Thomas noted that this game had been "the most important NFL playoff game in the long history of Mexican tourism." Jim Reeves, likewise, reminded Dallas fans to cancel their planned trip to Arizona in February (site of the Super Bowl), and also indicated that a good place to see Cowboy players would be in Mexico. Still, Tony did not apologize for what he did. Further, he did as Ramiro Sr. and his mom and dad would have expected him to do: he stood in front of the media, answered all their questions, and vowed to do better. Although disappointed, he stated that "I don't live with regrets. . . . I'm content in my own skin. If I try to be a good person, if I'm strong enough in my faith, if I'm strong enough in what I am trying to do, then I feel like I'm doing things the right way." So, a season that had held so much promise ended with a thud. As part of their summary, various reporters accorded Tony a grade of "B" for the year and got one more shot in for good measure. "He earned a contract extension and a second trip to the Pro Bowl. But [he] will be remembered more for another poor performance down the stretch and a trip to Cabo."[14]

While the 2007 season had many high and low points, there was an event off the field that touched Tony's life: Ramiro Jr. was diagnosed with prostate cancer. Tony, as would any son, expressed concern about his father's situation. "He's your dad. You've been close for so long; it can be a scary thing." The news broke just before the Bills game, and some questioned Tony's professionalism by claiming that his mind was on his dad's illness, not the game. Romo put a stop to such talk in short order. "You love your dad. You just want him to be all right. . . . It's a step in the path of life. Football's football. When you're on the field, that's all you think about." Fortunately, the cancer was found early on, and Ramiro's good physical condition also helped. Ramiro and Joan attended the game against the Patriots and a few months later, in January 2008, he was medically cleared. Ramiro then returned to two very important things: handling Tony's business affairs and playing golf, both on his own and with his son.[15]

In a very surprising turn of events, the underdog Giants went on to win Super Bowl XLII against the undefeated Patriots, in one of the biggest upsets in the game's history. The star of the day for New York was Eli Manning, the Giants' quarterback. Given that he guided his team to a title, there was now talk that Eli had passed Tony to become the best quarterback in the NFC. While local scribes might not have agreed with this notion, the belief certainly was out there among NFL fans. In February 2008, Jennifer Floyd Engel noted this in one of her columns, while also coming to Tony's defense. "There is this perception that being popular . . . is Romo's endgame, not Super Bowl glory. It is not true, and I say this as somebody who remembers Romo from the day he arrived [at camp] . . . ready to prove himself." Still, fans were starting to worry whether Tony, even with all his talent, would be able to lead Dallas to a title.[16]

As the start of the 2008 season approached, more comments appeared. Gil LeBreton went so far as to go back to Tony's time at EIU and mentioned that the Panthers made the playoffs all three years he started and lost in the first round each time. Get the point? "The man has never won a playoff game in his life." Overall, LeBreton argued, "It's been a spellbinding script—except for the playoff chapters." Still, others continued to focus on how hard Tony worked to improve himself. "He has spent the off-season working to become calmer in the pocket. Romo watched videotape of . . . Joe Montana in his glory years. . . . Romo's journey to the next level begins next week. . . . I expect it to be a good one."[17]

Once again, the season started with great promise. Tony threw for over 600 yards in the first two games of the year, against Cleveland and Philadelphia (both victories), then he headed home to Wisconsin, to take on the Packers yet again. Dallas defeated Green Bay 27–16 and Tony had a good game, completing 17 of 30 passes for 260 yards and one score (and one interception). As had happened before, area papers talked about how proud the hometown folks were of Romo, and how he gave back to his community. 2008 marked the fourth year Tony had been part of a youth football camp in Burlington. One of the young men who took part was Eric Dankle, who was a backup quarterback at BHS. His comments about the Dallas star say a lot about the type of person Tony is, for "he's pretty low-key. He's nothing to get real nervous about because he's just a normal player who came through here. He just kind of seems like one of us." Another comment by a former teacher supported Dankle's statement. "When you have a dignitary like that . . . it seems they're constantly watching their watch. . . . But Tony isn't afraid to do these kinds of things. He's just a quality young man."[18]

Dallas split its next two games, losing to Washington and beating Cincinnati. Next, they headed to Tempe to play the Cardinals. The Cowboys trailed 24–14 with about two minutes to go in the fourth quarter. Then, Marion Barber took a Romo pass 70 yards for a score. After holding Arizona, Dallas drove for a 52-yard field goal to tie as time expired. In overtime, however, all that could go wrong, did. On the first snap, the Cardinals sacked Tony, and he fumbled. Though Dallas recovered, their quarterback was injured on the play (a sprained right pinkie) and missed on his next two pass attempts. On fourth down, the Cowboys' punt attempt was blocked and returned for a touchdown. Final score: 30–24. The injury kept Romo out of action until the middle of November. In the meantime, Dallas lost two of the three games he missed.[19]

Tony shined upon his return to action, leading his club to three straight wins to move their record to 8–4. In two of those games, he threw for more than 330 yards. The contest against Seattle on Thanksgiving Day must have been very satisfying and helped him forget what happened in 2006. Dallas won, 34–9, and Tony threw for three touchdowns.[20] Then, as had happened in previous years, Dallas's fortunes turned negative once again and they lost two of their next three games, falling to the Steelers, beating the Giants, and losing at home to the Ravens. Now, at 9–6, Dallas faced a do-or-die situation yet again: playing the Eagles on the road for a wild-card spot. The winner moved on; the loser stayed home.

By halftime, there was no doubt which team was going to be out. After Dallas tied the score at 3–3 at the very end of the first quarter, the Eagles went on a 24–0 run (indeed, it would reach 41–0 by the end of the third quarter), as they crushed Dallas, 44–6. Tony threw for 183 yards, had one pick, was sacked three times, and suffered a rib injury. He later collapsed in the showers after the game. It is not an understatement to say that the day was a complete disaster. Although the Eagles outgained Dallas by only five yards (303 to 298), five turnovers, including two fumbles returned for scores, doomed any hopes. While most reporters recognized that this horrible result was not all Tony's doing, Gil LeBreton asked openly how much of this ruin was the quarterback's fault, saying, "three Decembers of Tony Romo have peeled open his flaws . . . his antsy feet, his propensity to be loose and breezy with the football . . . his inability to spread the passing game around." Another scribe, Rick Herrin, pointed out that Romo's record in

December games now stood at 5–10. In other words, he was not coming through at the most important times. Again, his figures for the year were quite good: 3,448 yards, 26 scores, 14 picks, and a 61 percent completion mark, but once more, the final goal was not reached. It was another sad end to a season.[21]

On the first day of 2009, Jim Reeves chimed in with his evaluation and focused on the way that Romo handled the press conference after the game. Tony was his usual humble self and promised to work harder to bring a title to Dallas. Still, he said in effect that this was not the end of the world and that the sun would come up tomorrow. Nothing wrong with that, but was this the right time to say it out loud? Reeves spoke for many upset fans who felt that Tony did not take the defeat gravely enough. "I seriously doubt that Cowboy fans were looking for a rational perspective from their quarterback at that point." Reeves and many Dallas fans continued to believe in Tony's abilities, but their patience was starting to wear thin.[22]

In 2009 things changed for the better, although again the Cowboys did not reach the Super Bowl. Tony had a terrific year on the field, topping his previous passing record, finishing with 4,483 yards.[23] He had 26 scores and only nine picks in leading Dallas to a division title with a record of 11–5. He had three games in which he threw for more than 300 yards, with his high (379) for the year coming in week 12 against the Giants in a 31–24 loss. Just like in 2008, Dallas closed out the year with a game against Philadelphia, although this game would take place in Texas. The rivals were playing for the division title and a home playoff date.

How much things changed in one year! On January 3, 2010, Dallas atoned for their loss the previous year by controlling every aspect of the game against Philadelphia. They won their division for the first time since 2007, won the last game of the season for the first time since 1999, and swept the Eagles for the first time since 2005. Just as severely as he had been decried after the 44–6 loss, Tony was praised after he completed 24 of 34 passes for 311 yards, including two touchdowns—certainly, a complete reversal from that awful night in 2008. After the victory Tony reflected by saying that "it's enjoyable definitely right now. Obviously, we have some history with the Eagles. . . . We haven't arrived, and we haven't accomplished anything. . . . There's hopefully a lot of season left." Surely, the time had, at last, come for Romo to guide his team to glory in the playoffs. The task would start again in one week, against the same, familiar, and hated foe in green, silver, and white.[24]

Of course, it would not have been correct for the local media to be fully confident going into the third contest against the Eagles. After all, Tony had lost in his two playoff starts, and it was important to keep these failures in mind. Still, the scribes had hope that this time, finally, things would be different. All involved, especially Jerry Jones and Tony Romo, knew the stakes. The win "has to happen or this season is no different than 2007, when a 13–3 regular-season followed by a quick playoff ouster didn't exactly define success." Tony tried to calm the fans' fears. "Those past games have absolutely no bearing on anything going forward. . . . I think we can play well as a team in January, but we've got to go out and do it. . . . And that's sort of what it comes down to. Doing it." With bated breath, the entire Dallas area awaited Wild Card Saturday on January 9, 2010.[25]

Just as had happened in their meeting in December 2008, this game was over by the half. The difference was that this time, it was the Cowboys who held the large lead. Tony had two scoring passes in the second quarter, and he also led three other drives for points (two field goals and a rushing touchdown). As the teams went to their locker rooms, the score stood at 27–7. The two teams then each scored single touchdowns in the third and fourth quarters, and Dallas won, 34–14. Romo threw for 244 yards and the two scores. He did not have an interception. The Cowboys' offense that day was well balanced; they also ran for almost 200 yards. After the game, Tony and his boss were overjoyed but also looked forward to bigger and better things. "I'm going to go out and work as hard as I can, and if we're good enough, we'll win. We'll find a way to get the job done." Jerry Jones felt that his fourth-year signal caller always gave his team a chance to win. "When you have a quarterback who plays like Tony . . . you'll find yourself winning the first [playoff], and you'll find yourself thinking that you've got a chance to win the next one and on from there." Now that Romo and his teammates had passed this hurdle, Minnesota was next in line. To add even more drama, the Vikings were now led by Brett Favre.[26]

It is no surprise that the upcoming contest made for good copy in the local papers. Here were two signal callers who played with a similar "gunslinger" style. Further, Favre had acted as a mentor to Romo, with the two sending each other text messages over the years. The big difference was that this would be Favre's 22nd playoff start, including two Super Bowls (and one victory in the big game), while Tony was still quite inexperienced. This was the first time he had gone beyond the first round in a playoff game at any level. The 19-year veteran went out of his way to praise the younger quarterback and advised him to keep doing what had brought him to this point. "He makes plays that other people wouldn't make, that other people wouldn't attempt to make, and that's what makes him a special player." Now, it was showdown time! Which one of them would lead their side to victory?[27]

As well as Dallas played the previous week was as poorly as they played against Minnesota. The purple gang applied great pressure all day long, and the Cowboys' offensive line did not protect Tony. The final score was 34–3. He was sacked six times and hit on 10 occasions. There was so much heat that of his 22 completions (on 35 attempts for 198 yards, and a pick), 16 went to either a tight end or a running back. What that means is that Tony often had to "check off" and "dump" passes because there was not enough time for his wide receivers to run their longer routes. In addition, Romo had three fumbles, two of which the Vikings recovered. After the game, he once again brought up the same points as his earlier end-of-season statements. "With this team, it is all about improvement. We didn't show a lot of that today, but we will take a lot of things from this game to find a way to improve on them and go forward." Would such words be enough to soothe the hurt feelings of Dallas fans?[28]

Of course, as Dallas exited the playoffs, there was bound to be grumbling. Tony had failed yet again, some said. A couple of days after the loss, Jennifer Floyd Engel came to the signal caller's defense in her column. Yes, she said, you could blame him, losing two fumbles and tossing an interception, but this writer chose to look at the positives, the most important one being that the team's quarterback had gotten the "can't win in the playoff" hex off his back. "These Cowboys will go into next season not having to answer for another playoff loss. Those issues are off the table." She then went on to praise Tony's leadership and work ethic. "His leadership is underrated: so is his game. . . . The only reason it [this game] was not uglier was because of Romo . . . he is the biggest building block of all." Small steps forward would finally, hopefully, lead to a Super Bowl win, right?[29]

Off the field, Tony once again had to deal with a medical issue, this time with his beloved grandfather. In a 2011 story in their hometown paper, the elder Romos talked about some of the problems Ramiro Sr. had confronted since 2007. He was feeling tired and weary all the time, and by the end of that year, he was diagnosed with a weak valve in his heart. A doctor in Dallas told Ramiro that he needed surgery but was too weak to survive the operation. It would take a new procedure, not developed until the summer of 2009, to save his life. Finally, Ramiro had his operation on November 19, 2009. He recalled, "Before we went into the operating room, my wife called all the doctors . . . and asked them if they would pray with us. . . . They asked God to bless their hands." After his surgery, Ramiro was able to leave the hospital after only three days. He would be able to continue his work for the Catholic Church as well as support his grandson through the ups and downs of all parts of his life. Once again, Tony's family had been blessed and an important member of the clan had survived a difficult situation.[30]

Tony, now seen as the team's foundation, had suffered injuries from time to time, but nothing that had kept him out for the better part of a season. The longest he had been out since becoming a starter were the three games he missed in the middle of 2008. If the Cowboys were to get past their frustrations, make it to a Super Bowl, and win, Romo had to be on the field and his offensive line had to protect him from taking too many severe hits. By the time training camp started, once again the talk was about going all the way to a title game in Dallas in the new Cowboys Stadium built by team owner, Jerry Jones. All the players and coaches said the right things in late July. Tony was respected by the other players, and his head coach believed that he was a member of the elite group of quarterbacks in the league. The figures backed up these claims. Going into 2010, Romo's mark as a starter stood at 38–17 (winning almost 70 percent of his games), he had taken Dallas to three playoff appearances, and now he had won a game in the postseason. Still, he needed to get "the ring" in order to solidify his legacy. The media also continued to stress how hard he worked on his mechanics, trying to make the smallest adjustments needed to improve his play. Surely, all this effort and analysis would pay off in the end?[31]

With the start of the new season nigh, the talk about representing the NFC in the Super Bowl continued into early September, even though the team sometimes struggled in the preseason (in which they finished 3–2). Jennifer Floyd Engel even went so far as to predict that the home team would be playing the Miami Dolphins in the big game in the facility known as "Jerry World." Interestingly, she mentioned that one of the biggest areas of concern would be the offensive line. Still, the argument was, there were no *great* teams in the NFC going into 2010, and the Cowboys were the best of the bunch. Now, they were ready to start the year going up against another bitter rival, the squad from our nation's capital. Tony looked forward to the challenge and hoped to start off well in the new year. "You know how it goes if you don't start winning football games. We have a tough schedule this year, so it's going to be a great test, but I think our team is up to the challenge."[32]

Unfortunately, things did not go well for Dallas in 2010, and they started off by losing four of their first five games.

They fell to Washington, then at home to the Bears; beat the Texans on the road; then lost to Tennessee at home and to the Vikings on the road. Tony had his best game of the year against the Titans, throwing for 406 yards and three scores, but he also had three interceptions and was sacked six times. In that game, the Cowboys also had one dozen penalties. Although they rolled up over 500 yards of total offense, the many mistakes cost Dallas the victory. The costliest one came after Tony threw a score to tie the game at 27–27, when a Cowboy got flagged for unsportsmanlike behavior. That meant the home team kicked off from their 15-yard line. The Titans' returner brought the ball all the way back to the Dallas 11, setting up the winning score. Tony followed this performance with another three scores, but also two more picks, in a 24–21 loss to Minnesota. Certainly, things could not get any worse, could they?[33]

Well, they did. Dallas next played the Giants at home and Tony got off to a good start. By early in the second quarter, he had already thrown for a touchdown and had completed five of his seven attempts. Then, a blitz by a New York linebacker drove Romo to the ground on his left shoulder, breaking his clavicle. This injury often requires surgery. At best, Jerry Jones believed that it would take somewhere between six and eight weeks for Tony to return to action. The final tally was not telling of how things went. The visitors led 38–20 when Dallas scored a couple of touchdowns in the last minutes of the game to make it a bit closer. After losing 41–35, the Cowboys stood at 1–5 and there was little hope left of making the playoffs. Tony's replacement, Jon Kitna, did a decent job and the team finished the season 6–10, winning five of their last eight games. Although the surgery went well, and Tony might have been able to play in the last two weeks of the season, there was no reason to put him in harm's way. The 2010 season was a lost cause, and it was time to focus on 2011. Once again, at the end of the year, Romo indicated he would work hard to make himself better and prepare for, hopefully, a rebound season.[34]

While the season on the field (and in the training room) proved difficult for the Dallas quarterback, things went well in his personal life. In 2009, he met Candice Crawford, who at the time was working as a sports broadcaster in the Dallas area. She was born in Lubbock and raised in the Dallas area. She attended the University of Missouri, graduating with a degree in journalism. As with many first dates, there was a bit of awkwardness when Tony asked Candice to go out. Indeed, he used a bit of sleight-of-hand, telling her that "a group" of people were going to a movie, asking if she wanted to tag along. She agreed but did not know that Romo was only interested in having the two of them on the date. When he picked her up, he casually said that all the other members of the party had, unexpectedly, "dropped out." Thus began their courtship. Candice also had to deal with some issues herself as she had a difficult time getting her parents, huge Cowboy fans, not to come out to meet the team's starting quarterback. Likely she did not want her mom and dad to fawn too much over Tony. Things worked out between them and, by 2011, the couple was engaged, and by May of that year, they married.[35]

Of course, the impending marriage of a media "power couple" drew the attention of both Dallas and Wisconsin newspapers. The Texas-based stories focused on how Tony was handling the upcoming nuptials while still leading fellow veterans in practice. Not surprisingly, he was asked about what made him more nervous: facing down NFL defenders, or marriage. Tony playfully responded, "I don't know. It's coming up, so we'll see." By the time the newlyweds went north for Romo's annual football camp in Burlington, he was more direct: "Getting married was fun. . . . We took a week . . . and had a good time." Still, the Romos were committed to the camp in Tony's hometown. "I get to talk to the kids and give back some knowledge I've learned. . . . We keep getting great numbers, and kids keep coming back. I get to give back to the community a little bit. It's great."[36]

Although Tony's marriage was a nice side story, eventually the sport scribes turned their attention back to the field of play and the hoped-for improvement by the Cowboys for the 2011 season. The new year would be the first full year for new head coach Jason Garrett, who replaced Wade Phillips after the team's 1–7 start in 2010. Tony was certain that things would be better, saying that, "I'll tell you what, this team is going to play good football next year. We are going to be competitive. We won't have a season like we had last year." Of course, writers such as Jennifer Floyd Engel were not quite convinced. The writer even noted in her column that she was embarrassed when she said the words "How do you figure that?" accidentally during a visit with Romo. The overall theme of the team in early 2011 was "change," and how to turn things around from the losing season the previous year.[37]

As the calendar moved toward the fall, the criticism about the team and its field general became more and more biting. Mac Engel, on the other hand, advised his readers that there had been many quarterbacks in the NFL who did not win a Super Bowl until they were in their 30s (Tony was now 31). He expressed confidence that this signal caller might join the group that included the likes of Peyton Manning and John Elway. Still, the writer argued, it was time for him to step up and move beyond the lone playoff win against the Eagles. In part, Engel's argument was based on the fact that for many years Dirk Nowitzki, the great forward for the Dallas Mavericks, had failed to lead his team to an NBA title. Well, that drought ended in June 2011. In short, the "other" big star in Dallas had brought home a title. Would Tony be able to do likewise?[38]

Were all the failures since 2006 Romo's fault? No one with any sense of how football is played would make that argument. Still, the fans were getting restless. Just before the start of preseason games, Randy Galloway did his best to remind folks, many of whom were impressed with the leadership of Jon Kitna (it is always great to be the backup quarterback when things are not going well, right?) during the nine games he started while Tony was injured, that Dallas's best chance to win still depended on having #9 in the huddle. "Past failures are well documented, but that's not always Romo's fault, even if he receives most of the blame when things continually go wrong." It takes the effort of all involved to win a Super Bowl, and Galloway argued that Dallas was still short in many areas. Still, the quarterback position was not a position of need for the Cowboys going into 2011. "At this moment in this training camp, it'd be a ridiculous stretch to say the Cowboys have the necessary pieces. . . . But the quarterback is certainly capable."[39]

Heading to the end of the preseason, an important concern continued to be whether the offensive line would protect their starter and make it possible to keep him in all the team's games. For 2011, Tony would be starting behind three new linemen, including a new center, as Andre Gurode, who had started at that position in 59 of Romo's 61 starts, was cut. He would be replaced by Phil Costa. The other two new members of the line were rookies. When asked if he was concerned about playing behind such an untested group, Tony was calm and indicated that this was just part of playing in the NFL. Players would come, and players would go, and the veteran quarterback believed in his teammates. "We need these young guys to step up and play. They've been working hard. It's their opportunity." In many ways, Tony's statement must have had him looking back to his early days in Dallas, when he was the one who had to prove himself.[40]

The first game of the season featured a good performance, numbers-wise, on Tony's part, as he threw for 342 yards and two scores (with one very costly interception). The new offensive line had its problems and gave up four sacks. In addition, Romo fumbled the ball as the offense was on the Jets' 2-yard line. At that moment, the Cowboys led, 24–17. A score would have likely sealed the win. Later, with the game tied at 24, and around 30 seconds to go (after Tony's interception a few seconds earlier), New York kicked a field goal to take the lead. A final desperate pass and a lateral ended on the Dallas side of the field, and the Cowboys lost, 27–24. An article by Randy Galloway summed up the frustration felt by both the fans and the reporters. "Two Blunders by Romo Make All the Difference" is not a headline any player would like to see. As always, Tony accepted responsibility when he did not play well: "I cost us the game." "Yes, you did," responded Galloway. So, after just one game was it possible that this was going to be yet another lost season?[41]

The week after such a heartbreaking loss can be difficult, and many in town now firmly believed the Dallas starter could simply not win in the clutch. Well, he proved them wrong the very next game. Dallas reversed the score from the Jets game, this time winning, 27–24. Tony threw for 345 yards and two scores. What was most impressive, however, was the fact that of the 33 passes attempted, only two were while he was healthy. A blitz by a San Francisco linebacker on just the third play of the game resulted in a cracked rib. Tony did not receive medical attention until halftime. Further, Dallas trailed by 10 points in the final quarter, before Tony returned to lead their rally. The game was tied after regulation, and then Romo completed a 77-yard pass to set up the game-winning score in overtime. This was the type of performance that other players, fans, and even the team owner could draw encouragement from. As Jerry Jones noted, "This has to be one of those things that will follow him through his career. . . . I know he had to wait a little while before [the painkillers] took hold. But, boy, did he come back. That was inspirational."[42]

Shortly after this moving win, Tony was featured in another story designed to inspire. September is National Hispanic Heritage month, and a story on the ESPN website recounted many aspects of the Romo family history covered in this book. Ramiro and Joan, the article mentioned, were in San Francisco and greeted their injured son shortly after the victory against the 49ers. As part of the commemorations of Latinos playing in the NFL, Tony's parents proudly noted how often they saw their boy's jersey when they visited relatives in Coahuila. "We get a kick out of it every time. It just goes to show the fans appreciate what he does on the football field." Tony certainly understood what he meant to the Spanish-surnamed fans of the Cowboys, a team with a substantial number of such *fanáticos*. "The Cowboys have such a strong Hispanic base, you can't help but see the number of fans that support us. . . .

It's awesome to be part of a team that gets that support, and I really appreciate the support they give us."[43]

The rest of the season was, to say the least, a roller-coaster ride. By the midpoint, Dallas was a .500 team. Then, they won three games in a row, moving them to 7–4. In one game, against Buffalo, Tony was almost perfect: completing 23 of 26 attempts for 270 yards and three touchdowns. Dallas won, 44–7. The last game in this winning stretch was a 20–19 win over the Miami Dolphins on Thanksgiving Day. Then, as happened before, a late-season swoon kicked in and Dallas lost four of their final five games, with the only victory coming against Tampa Bay on December 17. Still, they had a chance to win the division title in—stop here if you have heard this before—the last game of the year against the Giants in New Jersey.[44]

In the week before going to New York, Tony was injured again in a game against the Eagles. As he was throwing a pass, his right hand hit against a defender's helmet. For a time, coaches thought he had broken his hand. While the Cowboys lost that game, 20–7, the good news was that this was not a fracture, and Tony would, after some rehabbing, be able to play in the game for the division crown.[45]

As game day neared, fans were reminded of the disaster that took place in 2008 when the Cowboys travelled to Philadelphia in a similar winner-take-all game for the NFC East crown. Reporters also stated that Dallas had lost six of their last eight to the Giants, including blowing a 12-point lead in a home game against New York earlier that December. Still, all the players said the "right" things about the team's chances going into the game. Tight end Jason Witten remarked that "This is a one-game opportunity. We believe we are a good team. . . . It's just a matter of executing." One positive on the Cowboys' side was that

Tony was "playing the best football of his career" before his bruised hand against the Eagles. As a caveat to Tony, one scribe noted that "legacies and reputations could be upheld or altered by the outcome" of this game. While Clarence Hill was talking about the entire club, one could not help but think that the main object of this statement was the man under center, the one who had only one playoff victory to his credit.[46]

As happened in decisive games in earlier years, Dallas was pretty much done by halftime and trailed, 21–0. To their credit, they did make a push, closing the score to 21–14 with less than 10 minutes to go in the fourth quarter. With just under six minutes to go, however, the Giants kicked a field goal to take a two-possession lead, then added a touchdown with just under four minutes left to close out a 31–14 win.[47] For a change, the local media did not place the blame on Romo. Tony passed for 289 yards, two scores, and one interception. This was his first pick since the game against Miami back on Thanksgiving Day. There was plenty of blame to go around, however. The offensive line gave up six sacks and the Giants pressured Tony all day long. Meanwhile, the Dallas defense did not put much pressure on Eli Manning. Also, the Cowboys' leading rusher amassed a mere 30 yards. All in all, it was another disappointing end to a season that started, as most years do in Dallas, with talk of at least the playoffs, if not the Super Bowl. Gil LeBreton described the end of Romo's sixth season under center this way: The team, "they're 8–8. A tease, but ultimately [an] unsatisfying pretender. They are average—not, as the owner said, 'very good.'" Tony summed up the loss by saying, "The guys fought really hard to get back in this football game. It's not a good feeling right now. . . . You put so much time and effort into being out there and playing your best. . . . We need to continue to get better and improve, and we will this off-season."[48]

In his end-of-season grades, Clarence Hill gave Tony an A for the season. He certainly did the best he could to help Dallas, as Tony had 31 touchdowns and only 10 picks. He completed 66.2 percent of his passes and threw for 4,184 yards. That type of season usually earns a quarterback a chance to play in the postseason, but once again, the Cowboys fell short. In sum, Tony Romo had now played one-half of his career and had done well. He was recognized as one of the best quarterbacks in the NFL, but the playoff/big game jinx continued to haunt him. As he moved into what would be the last six years of his time in Dallas, Tony continued to seek not personal glory but the chance to win a title for the rabid Cowboy fans throughout the nation.[49]

CHAPTER 8

TONY'S TIME ON THE FIELD RUNS OUT, 2012–2017

Stop here if you have heard this before. After losing to the Giants in a winner-take-all contest on New Year's Day of 2012, the Cowboys returned to Texas to, one more time, lick their wounds and promise to do better. Yet another season with as many losses as wins was not what fans (or the players or Jerry Jones) had hoped for. A quick look at the offensive and defensive numbers of the team showed that they were exactly what their record proved: a middle-of-the-pack team. While Tony had an excellent year, Dallas ranked 15th (of 32 teams) in scoring with a figure of 23.1. On the other side of the ball, they gave up 21.7 points per game, 16th in the league. Ordinary numbers for a humdrum squad.[1]

Still, at least among some, the griping got louder and louder in regard to the team as a whole, as well as in their analysis of the quarterback position. By February, there was new talk about how Tony was not in the same league as his Giants' foe, Eli Manning. Of course, the facts that New York, once again, won the Super Bowl (defeating the Patriots, 21–17, on February 5), and now Manning had two rings, while Romo had but one playoff win, did not help the situation. Just a few days after the title game, for example, there was a story in a Fort Worth paper that mentioned how impressed Tiger Woods was with Tony's golf game. "He understands how to play. . . . He can really move the ball." Well, this was just too much for reporter Randy Galloway to bear as he noted the poor timing "for Tiger to be offering glowing praise for, yes, Tony's golf game. The dang Giants just won the Super Bowl. That dang Eli did it again."[2]

How could Dallas improve in order to be playing football, not golf, in early February? Well, yet again, ownership tinkered with the coaching staff. For 2012, the team brought in Bill Callahan to serve as the new offensive line coach. If you remember, an important aspect of the last game of the prior season was Tony under heavy pressure by the Giants. Overall, he endured 36 sacks that year. Over the off-season Dallas spent a lot of money in order to try to improve this part of their team. All of this was done because, as owner Jones noted, "It's been disappointing to not have been in the Super Bowl in these key years of Romo's career."[3]

Going into 2012 Tony had other things on his mind besides the never-ending drive to improve on-field performance. First, Candice was expecting the Romos' first child. She gave birth to a son, Hawkins, in April. Next, the large contract he signed back in 2007 would expire at the end of the 2013 season. Had Romo done enough to merit a new contract that would keep him among the highest paid quarterbacks in the NFL? Jerry Jones and his son Stephen (who serves as vice president of the team) certainly thought so. Both believed that the Cowboys had an elite quarterback and they needed to provide help for him on both sides of the ball. Indeed, Stephen argued that "There are not many better than him out there." Still, father and son also realized that "he hasn't gotten it done yet [but]. . . . Every year he improves. As he gets better, our chances get better." The team, then, would focus on making the offensive line as strong as possible, as well as bringing in more help for the defense through the draft. If they did that, it was thought, then Dallas would be closer to its ultimate goal. Finally, as he always did, Tony returned to Burlington to run his football camp during the end of June.[4]

Despite all the effort and money spent, the results of 2011 did not change. For starters, the offensive line surrendered exactly the same number of sacks. The offense scored a few more points, but still finished 15th in the league (scoring 23.5 points per game). Things went downhill on the defensive side of the line (mostly because of a rash of injuries), however, as Dallas sank to 24th in the NFL, giving up a total of 400 points. Tony had some great games—he threw for over 400 yards three times: against the Giants on October 28, Washington on November 22, and finally versus New Orleans on December 23. Sadly, all these impressive performances came during defeats. Still, the Cowboys had a record of 8–7 going into the last game of the year, this time against the team from our nation's capital. Yet again, this was a winner-take-all contest that would decide the crown of the NFC East. Is this sounding eerily familiar? Tony had passed for 406 yards the previous week against the Saints though Dallas lost, 34–31 in overtime, but going into the game in DC local writers expressed concerns that even with such recent gaudy numbers, Romo could not win a big game.

Of course, football is a team sport, and writer Mac Engel knew this fact as he went on to list all the problems (such as injuries to the starters on the defensive side of the ball and continued issues with the offensive line) Dallas faced. Additionally, the home team had won six games in a row and featured a great quarterback, Baylor's own Robert Griffin III. Engel knew it was not fair to put all the blame for past defeats on Tony, but he also stressed that the Cowboys' signal caller *had* to come through in games like this to change people's views. There would be only so many chances in a career to prove doubters wrong. The scribe summed up what had to happen: "The Cowboys have to win . . . to change [the idea] that Romo is always going to be just slightly not good enough . . . tonight, Tony Romo has to be the best player on the field." Engel titled his article, "It Can't be the Same Old Story."[5]

Only it was. Dallas lost, 28–18, and Tony had a bad game: he threw for only 196 yards and had three interceptions. The last one was the killer as the Cowboys had closed to 21–18. There is no need to go into specifics, only to say that, even after another crushing loss, the Joneses and Coach Garrett continued to say they believed in their quarterback though his mark as a starter in win-or-go-home games now stood at 1–6. Garrett noted after the loss that "I think you have to understand the whole body of work. He's done a lot of great things for this franchise. We're excited about him being our quarterback." It was getting a bit more difficult for fans to share this belief. Sure, Tony threw for 4,903 yards, but his touchdowns declined to 28 and his picks increased to 19. The results: 8–8 and no playoffs. These figures earned him a grade of D from the local media at their end-of-season recap. Would 2013 be any different?[6]

As the Cowboys headed into a new season, they continued to make moves. There was one major difficulty, however. The team's salary setup was creating a problem known as limited cap space, making it hard to sign free agents.

In a nutshell, Tony's salary as Dallas's highest paid player left the team with little money to spend in order to bring in outside help. Thus, the team began to let go of some other players and eventually freed up around $7 million of funds. While that might sound like a lot of money, in the high-stakes world of the NFL, it really is not. What the team needed to do was to deal with how Romo's pay counted against the total salaries paid to their roster. In other words, the club could only pay so much to all their players, and Tony's salary had to be reworked so as to give Dallas wiggle room to sign free agents to, hopefully, produce better results.[7]

Although Tony had one more year on his current contract, if he signed a new agreement the team would be able to clear cap space and make it possible to sign new players. In a very harsh column, Randy Galloway was critical of Romo for, in his view, not being willing to take a team-friendly deal that would have allowed him to get paid while also making it possible for the Cowboys to have more cap room. With a bit of sarcasm, the reporter noted that "the fact that Tony skated this week on the opportunity to score public perception points continues a long personal trend. . . . In reality, you won't find a more devoted team guy. It's just that Tony doesn't want you to know it."[8] A very sarcastic tone, indeed! During the 2013 season, and under very difficult conditions, Tony would demonstrate just how much of a team player he really was.

A few days after this column appeared, the team and Tony reached a new deal. It would be for six years and could net him $108 million, including a bonus of $25 million, for signing. Of that figure, the Cowboys guaranteed their quarterback $55 million. This means that he would earn that amount even if he did not complete the contract (which would end in 2019). Immediately, there was debate as to whether Tony was worth such a huge sum. In the article announcing the agreement, two local reporters presented both the positives and negatives of the results of the quarterback's career so far. Going into 2013, Tony ranked first in team history with a completion percentage of 64.7percent and touchdown passes (with 177). Overall, he had a record as a starter of 55–38 (a winning percentage of nearly 60 percent). That is not a bad record at all. However, the scribes also argued that not only was Tony's mark 17–21 over the past three years, and 1–3 in playoff games, but the Cowboys had not made the playoffs since 2009. "Still, the Cowboys have great faith in Romo, believing he is their quarterback of not only the present but the future." This amount of money put him in the same league as players such as Aaron Rodgers, Drew Brees, and, of course, Tom Brady. But, the writers pointed out, the big difference was that all of these other signal callers had won Super Bowls. Jerry Jones certainly continued to support Tony. "He has a proven veteran . . . grasp of the intellectual side of the game. . . . He knows how to win games and has done it in a lot of different settings and under a lot of difficult circumstances."[9]

For Dallas, the 2013 season played out with disappointing results and the team finished with an 8–8 mark yet again. Still, they went into the last game of the season against the hated Eagles with—you guessed it—a chance to win the NFC East. Tony had another good statistical season, passing for 3,828 yards and 31 scores with only 10 picks. The offensive line continued to be a problem, however, giving up 35 sacks. There were, of course, some great games. For example, on October 6, against the Broncos in Texas, Tony threw for 506 yards and five scores. It was not enough: Dallas lost, 51–48.[10] Another highlight was his performance against the Packers on December 15 in which he threw for 358 yards and two scores. However, one of his two picks helped fuel Green Bay's rally from down 23–3 to a 37–36 victory. As the local paper noted, this was another "Tony moment" that he had to bounce back from. He would have an opportunity to do so the following week against Washington. It was in this game that Romo demonstrated his grit and determination to help his team.[11]

The 15th game of the 2013 season was vital to the Cowboys' hopes for a playoff spot. Things did not start off well, as a hit on Romo injured his back and hobbled him for most of the second half. To make matters worse, Dallas trailed 23–14 early in the fourth quarter. A short field goal by Dan Bailey brought them closer, at 23–17, and the defense stopped the home team, forcing a punt with less than four minutes left. Then, the Cowboys' offense took over at their 13-yard line: 87 yards away from the score that would keep their season alive. Tony guided the team down the field, completing passes of 51 and 17 yards. Eventually, Dallas got to the Washington one-yard line, where a running play lost nine yards. Now, it was fourth and goal from the 10. Would this result in another bitter defeat? Not this time: Tony threw a scoring strike to DeMarco Murray with around one minute left. The extra point sealed the victory, 24–23. Just as the local press had chided Tony after the Green Bay loss, they now heaped praise, saying he went from goat to hero in a span of one week. Again, Dallas had a chance to make the postseason. The one major issue was the condition of Tony's back. He would undergo a test when the team returned to Texas to see if he could play in the next game.[12]

While the game against Washington might have been Tony's finest hour so far, it came at a great cost; the tests on his back showed a severe injury that required surgery. The team's doctors did what they could to try to make it possible for Romo to play, but it was no use. On December 27 the Dallas starter had his operation and would be out for the rest of the year. Now, Tony would not get a chance to lead his team in yet another do-or-die game. As owner Jerry Jones noted, "You know him, we know him, and we know where his heart is. . . . It was a real superhuman effort for him to have finished the game the other day and made the plays to get us here." So much for not sacrificing for his squad. While the team rallied behind backup Kyle Orton, who threw for 358 yards and two scores (along with two interceptions), Dallas came up just short, losing to the Eagles, 24–22. Even more heartbreaking was the fact that Dallas had a chance to tie the game with a two-point conversion with less than four minutes to go, but the attempt failed. That wrapped up the 2013 season. At the end-of-year review, the local writers graded Romo's performance this year as a B. Not a bad grade, but they argued that "he didn't have the success that his contract and numbers suggest."[13]

Toward the end of the 2013 campaign, an article by S. L. Price appeared in *Sports Illustrated*, tracing Tony Romo's rise to fame in the NFL. Much of that information we have already covered, but there was one section that does need to be fleshed out. Part of the essay dealt with how Tony would be viewed if he did not win a title. Direct and honest as ever, he stated that not winning a Super Bowl ring, "You just can't be considered one of the best without it. Only some people can. . . . Everybody else, it comes down to that. Is it unfair? It doesn't matter. It is what it is. So you'd better go do it." Even after all the years of frustration and the big new contract, especially the last three 8–8 seasons, the drive still burned within Romo. Would he be able to make this happen, particularly now after major surgery on his back?[14]

Of course, a lot of what was written about Tony during the off-season dealt with his back and concerns about how well he would play in 2014. Jerry Jones spent most of that time trying to calm fans' fears. In late January, he noted that "I talk to Tony frequently, and so he's feeling much better. . . . How he's feeling, and how he's responding, is very good." Such accounts did not put to rest all doubts, and about two weeks after Jones' statement, Mac Engel suggested that it would be wise if the Cowboys were to secure a quarterback in the upcoming April draft. Engel went so far as to suggest that it would be wise to take a chance on another Eastern Illinois Panther, Jimmy Garoppolo (he would wind up with the Patriots). The notion was that time was starting to run out on the Romo era, and it would be smart to begin bringing along a youngster. Still, the team's leaders insisted that all was right with Romo's back and he was on schedule to return for the fall. Again, Jerry Jones stated that "Is he doing the throwing motion? Yes. Is he out there throwing to receivers right now? No. He is not throwing to receivers." By early May fans heard directly from Tony, who assured them that all would be well. "There's no question in my mind, not only am I going to be able to make it through 16 games, I'll make it through another five years. . . . I'm going to come back a better player than I've ever been."[15] Tony had even more incentive to come back and do well, and Candice gave birth to a second son, Rivers, in March 2014.

The Cowboys did their best to protect Tony during the preseason and limited his action on the field. For example, in the first preseason game, he did not play at all. In the second game, he took only 16 snaps. They also curbed his time on the practice field. All of this was done so as to have him as fresh and healthy as possible for the first game of the year on September 7 against San Francisco. Unfortunately, his performance against the 49ers did not go well. Tony threw for 281 yards and one score but had three interceptions. Immediately, there was talk that the Dallas coaching staff had not given Romo enough practice time and that he was not ready for the start of the year. Of course, Coach Garrett and teammates rallied to Tony's defense. Jason Witten, the tight end who started with the Cowboys the same year as his quarterback, was steadfast in his support. "He'll bounce back. He's got everybody's full support. He's the leader of this football team. He'll do that. He'll bounce back."[16]

And bounce back he did. Over the next month and a half, Tony guided the Cowboys to six straight wins, including triumphs on the road against strong clubs such as the Rams and Seahawks. All seemed, at long, long last, to be falling into place. Then came a home game against Washington on October 27. About midway through the third quarter, linebacker Keenan Robinson blitzed, hit the signal caller, and "folded Romo in half" with a knee to his back. Tony stayed on the ground for a long time as fans, teammates, coaches, and Jerry Jones all held their breath. He eventually got up and after negative X-rays in the locker room, took some pain medicine. The game was tied at 17–17 as Tony made his way back on to the field with about four minutes left in the fourth quarter. He did well after the injury, completing four of seven passes for 26 yards, but he did endure another sack and also fumbled. Eventually the visitors won, 20–17 in overtime. Overall,

Romo passed for over 200 yards on 17 of 28 attempts and had one score. While the loss stung, the bigger question was if he would be able to play the following week against the Cardinals. The team and Tony were hopeful, but further tests showed two small fractures in his back, so team doctors decided that he should not play.[17]

Dallas faltered against Arizona as backup Brandon Weeden did not play well and the Cowboys lost, 28–17. They were now 6–3 and had fallen out of first place in the NFC East. The following week's game would be against Jacksonville, but would take place in London, England. This was another game in which Tony showed his grit and team loyalty. He fought through the pain and helped to guide Dallas to a 31–17 win. After the long flight home, reporter Clarence Hill sang Romo's praises and called him a legend: "This is about accepting the truth about the best quarterback in Cowboys' history not named Troy Aikman or Roger Staubach." At Wembley Stadium, Tony completed 20 of 27 passes for 246 yards and three touchdowns. Receiver Dez Bryant summed up what the players felt about their quarterback by saying that "We all know the deal. And a lot of times he plays [in pain] like it doesn't even faze him. So we've just got to try to do that too." Hill summed up his thoughts of Tony by asking fans to "Appreciate him. Cherish him."[18]

The late season swoon that had taken place in earlier years did not occur in 2014, and Dallas cruised to the NFC East title. They clinched the title on December 21 with a 42–7 win against Indianapolis. In this game, Tony had the highest percentage of completed passes by any Cowboy quarterback in history, passing for 218 yards and four scores on 18 of 20 attempts. For good measure, Dallas then whupped Washington on the last day of the season, 44–17.

Tony's play inspired at least one teammate to say that he deserved to be the league's most valuable player (MVP). Quite a turnaround from previous years! Although Romo did not win the MVP—that honor went to Aaron Rodgers of the Packers—he put up great numbers and, more importantly, ended the five-year playoff drought. Up next would be the Detroit Lions in a first-round game in Texas.[19]

Shortly before the game against Detroit, David Flores caught up with [as] Ramiro Sr. and Felicita to get their take on Tony's season. As in previous interviews, the proud *abuelo* and *abuela* were thrilled to talk about their famous *nieto*. Ramiro opined that "The difference between this season and the other years is that Antonio has never had a team like this around him. He's never had this kind of help. He's more relaxed now because the Cowboys have a better overall team." Tony told his grandfather that he still believed that he would guide Dallas to the promised land. "Grandpa, we're going to win the Super Bowl one of these years." As always, the patriarch and matriarch of the clan expressed sincere gratitude for the opportunities that this country had provided them. Mr. Flores summed up the story by noting that "a Mexican immigrant would someday have a grandson playing quarterback for one of pro football's iconic franchises, Ramiro Sr. said, is a testament to the American dream. 'I worked hard and was able to provide for my family. This is still the country of opportunity, and Tony's career is proof of that.'"[20]

As the Cowboys prepared for their foes from Michigan, everyone said all the right things. Tony noted that "you're not guaranteed anything once you get there [to the playoffs]." Gil LeBreton chimed in with his thoughts about moving from a paper in Baltimore to come to Dallas, and how he had been told that he'd probably get a chance to cover a lot of Super Bowls "since the Cowboys seem to go every other year." The scribe then went on to remind fans about what happened in Seattle, and how things had gone in the following years. Yes, everyone was pumped about being in the playoffs but wary of outcomes from the recent past. On paper, Dallas was the better team, but then, we had all heard this story before. With the score 17–7 in favor of the visitors at the half, it is not too much of a stretch to think that many of the 91,000 fans in the stadium thought, "Here we go again." Indeed, Detroit kicked a field goal about midway through the third quarter and the score now stood at 20–7. Then, Dallas went on an 80-yard drive to cut the lead down to 20–14 with just less than three minutes to go in the period. A field goal early in the final stanza brought them within three points, and finally, Tony hit Terrance Williams with an eight-yard strike to round out the scoring with 2:32 left in the game. The final was 24–20. Overall, Romo had a great game and came through in the clutch. He completed 19 of 31 passes for 293 yards and two scores. This was a huge moment in Tony's life, as well as that of Coach Garrett. As Mac Engel noted, "This had been the type of 'big game' where these two men had shrunk and would 'never win' because they never had." Next, aptly, Tony would lead his team into Lambeau Field in Green Bay.[21]

Sadly, things did not turn out the way Dallas fans would have hoped. Certainly, the chance was there for the Cowboys. Aaron Rodgers was injured and could not move around very much. Also, the weather was "great" as far as early January in Green Bay, with the temperature at a "warm" 23 degrees. Additionally, Tony played very well. For once, the doubters could not place the blame of a defeat on him. Indeed, he showed his mettle again as he played with a torn ligament in his left ring finger. Overall, he completed 15 of 19 passes, two scores, and no picks. Behind 26–21 with just less than five minutes left, the Cowboys were driving toward the Packers' goal. Tony threw a deep ball to Dez Bryant who, it seemed, caught the ball, and made a move to reach toward the goal line. The ball then popped out of Bryant's hand, and he rolled on top of it just short of the end zone. The officials ruled it a catch, and Dallas had first and goal on the Green Bay 1-yard line. But the Packers appealed, and the pass was eventually ruled incomplete. There was much arguing by the Cowboys, but the call stood. Ultimately, they did not score and lost.[22] To no one's surprise, the local press gave Tony a grade of A for his season's effort. He threw for 3,705 yards, 34 scores, and only nine picks. Overall, a great year, but also one with great heartbreak at the very end. Once again, he was named to the Pro Bowl. He had proven that his back surgery was successful and that maybe, just maybe, 2015 (less a bad judgement call by an official) would finally be the year where Romo and Dallas would reach the Super Bowl.[23]

The lead-up to training camp in 2015 was, to say the least, a lot quieter than the previous year. Indeed, one of the most extensive stories on Tony over the off-season dealt with "old" quarterbacks reaching, and winning, the Super Bowl. Given the results of the 2014 season, hopefully, Romo might be the next member of this list, joining the likes of Brady, Peyton Manning, John Elway, and others. Otherwise, going into camp at the end of July, the talk centered around how regular Tony's participation would be in the preparation for the upcoming season. He also was busy with other pursuits: he had visits with late-night talk and award shows, a small part in a movie, commercials for Pizza Hut and DirectTV, and signed a deal to endorse

Under Armour.[24] Nothing like a successful season and not having to worry about his back to make for a pleasant summer! The team also had a lot of positive hype going into the season, and there was talk of a Super Bowl run. However, reporter Clarence Hill did note one troubling trend: "Not since the team won its last Super Bowl in 1996 have the Cowboys followed a double-digit win season with a successful campaign the following year. . . . Can the Cowboys reverse the curse?"[25]

The 2015 season started off spectacularly and seemed to herald a sequel to 2014. The Cowboys outgained the Giants 201 to 86 in the first half, dominated the time of possession almost 22 minutes to 8, yet trailed 13–6 at the intermission. They were still behind 23–13 and 26–20 in the fourth quarter, with the last score by New York coming with 1:34 left in the game. Then, Tony went to work. The game climaxed with a Romo to Witten 11-yard scoring strike to give Dallas a 27–26 win. As noted in a newspaper article the day after the contest, this marked the 24th time that Tony had led the Cowboys on either a fourth quarter or overtime drive to secure a win. In the decisive frame, Tony went 11 of 12 for 148 yards and two touchdowns. Overall, he finished with 356 yards and three scores along with two interceptions. Gil LeBreton called this come-from-behind effort a highly positive "chapter in the Tony Romo story." Suddenly, instead of asking if Romo could come through in crunch time, the feeling around town and in the local media was that he would always come through. Perhaps this marked the start of another special season?[26]

Then, in the blink of an eye, all these hopes crashed and burned. While the Cowboys did lose Dez Bryant to a broken foot in the New York game, an even greater misfortune awaited the team in the next contest, against the Eagles.

Dallas would win, 20–10, against their bitter rivals, but it would be costly indeed. As the Cowboys drove down to the Philadelphia 33, Tony dropped back to pass and was hit by Jordan Cox. He fumbled (recovered by the Eagles), but as he hit the turf, he felt a pop from his shoulder. It was the sound of his clavicle (also known as the collar-bone) breaking. It was now up to Brandon Weeden to keep things going. Mac Engel did not express much confidence in the situation as he noted that "the best the Cowboys can be without Romo is .500, and that will be a smashing suc-cess."[27] The reality of the situation would not come close to this guess. Dallas would go on to lose its next seven games. What had started out with so much promise, a 2–0 start, now turned to a 2–7 nightmare.

Dallas's starter would not return until the tenth game of the year, against the Miami Dolphins in a rainy South Florida. Remarkably, the Cowboys still had a chance for the playoffs, but they had to win all of the seven games that remained. Now that Tony was back, there was at least talk along these lines. Would this be possible, given that Romo had missed two months? Well, while he did not make every play, he did enough to guide Dallas to a 24–14 win. It might not have been pretty, but after seven straight losses, not too many were going to complain. Overall, Tony finished 18 of 28 for 227 yards with two scores and two picks. Even more amazingly, now at 3–7, Dallas stood only two games behind the NFC East division lead. Could there have been a miracle in the works? The following game would be a tall order indeed, as the Cowboys returned home to play on Thanksgiving Day against Carolina, a team whose record stood at 10–0.[28]

The joyous return to the field ended with a thud, unfor-tunately, against the Panthers, as the team from Charlotte ran roughshod over Dallas, winning 33–14. Tony showed a lot of rust in the first two quarters, as he threw three interceptions. By halftime, the game was pretty much out of reach as the visitors led, 23–3. In the third quarter, the deficit ballooned to 30–6, and after the most recent Panther score Tony came in to lead the offense. That series lasted only two plays for him when, on a tackle by Thomas Davis—you guessed it—the left collarbone snapped again. This time, it meant that Romo, most likely, was done for the year, and so were any hopes of making the playoffs. A few days later, doctors confirmed the worst possible news for Tony and Cowboys fans. The season was a disaster, as the team went 1–11 with three backup quarterbacks and finished 4–12 overall. Local reporters emphasized the need to get better backups, while Tony and the Joneses continued to argue that Romo still had some good years left, even as he would turn 36 in April 2016.[29]

During the off-season there was constant talk about Dallas's need for a new quarterback, at least a better backup, or a young player to develop as the next starter in a post-Romo era. Jerry Jones, on the other hand, continued to talk about Tony as his starter for the next few years. If there was a quarterback available, would Dallas take such a player? Romo himself chimed in that his surgery had gone well, that he was healing and would be ready. Okay, we've heard all of that before. All these themes occupied the minds and hearts of Cowboys fans up to the start of training camp. Before then, however, the NFL had its annual draft. Dallas had it highest pick in the first round since 1991, and they took running back Ezekiel Elliot of Ohio State. With much less fanfare and with little notice from the local media, with the 135th pick in the fourth round, Dallas selected Dak Prescott, a quarterback from

Mississippi State University. It wasn't until a few days after the draft that we got to hear the first talk about Prescott being a possible successor to Romo. Dak, of course, said all the right things going into the clubhouse. "Romo wins, and I win. I think that's the biggest thing you can take from the quarterback position. . . . To come to the Cowboys and learn under him will be exciting." It seems as if it was 2003 all over again, and a rookie needs to know his place in the pecking order.[30]

From the start of training camp, Prescott impressed the Dallas coaching staff. After the third preseason game, he had the highest passing rating of any quarterback in the NFL. Sure, that sounds fine, but he was playing against mostly non-starters. However, an event in that third contest, against the Seahawks, made it all the more necessary to continue to see what the rookie could do. You see, yet another terrible thing happened to Tony Romo in Seattle: another broken bone in his back. He was tackled by Cliff Avril and broke a vertebra. Surgery would not be necessary, but he would be out, at the very least, until late October or early November; that meant he would miss at least eight or nine regular season games. Given that Prescott was playing so well, Mac Engel asked the question that many did not want to hear. If Tony were able to return midseason, "Can you imagine the controversy if Dak is playing well?"[31]

What Engel foretold is exactly what happened. Dallas lost its first game of the year, 20–19, to New York, then, with Prescott playing brilliantly, the team ripped off eight straight wins. As we noted earlier, it is not usually accepted that a player, particularly a starting quarterback, should lose his place due to an injury. When Tony returned to practice 10 weeks after his injury, the question became this: bring in the veteran as the starter, or go with the hot hand that has had so much success? The answer was obvious. In a business such as professional football, you go with the player who is leading you to wins; that meant that Tony would now be the backup. By the end of November, Dallas was 9–1 and Romo accepted the reality of his situation. This was now Dak's team, and it was rolling. This was not an easy moment in Romo's life and career. Still, given all that he had learned from his grandparents and parents, he was as gracious as possible. As one reporter noted, after Tony did not take questions at a press conference, this was "likely proof of how hard it was for him to stand up and make concessions." He would return to the team roster in the eleventh week of the season. He finally had a chance to play in the final game of the season on New Year's Day, 2017. By that time, the team had won the NFC East, had a record of 13–2, and was preparing for the playoffs. Mac Engel noted in an article that the Cowboys had to get Tony into this game. The scribe, as probably most fans, did not want their last vision of Romo to be his being sacked and injured versus Seattle. Tony had earned the right to have, hopefully, a more positive outcome. "Let him walk away as a Dallas Cowboy with a good memory on the field rather than one standing on the sideline." And play he did, as Tony entered the game with the score tied at 3–3 early in the second quarter. He promptly guided his team on an 81-yard touchdown drive and finished it off with a three-yard scoring pass to Terrance Williams. The fact that Dallas lost 27–13 was really not important. This would be the final play of Tony's career. The Cowboys would lose to the Green Bay Packers in the first round of the playoffs the very next week, 34–31, thus ending their season.[32]

While there was a lot of discussion about Tony's future, it was all but certain that he would not wear a Cowboys' jersey again. The question was whether he would play at all in 2017. By late March, there was talk that he would be released, although Dallas did seek a possible trade. While Tony continued to have ties to the Joneses, he broke off his contact with Coach Garrett. A report in April indicated that he was mad at his former head coach because he did not give him a chance to regain his starting job.[33]

The final act in this play came on April 4. Tony retired and quickly took a job with CBS Sports to serve as the network's lead NFL analyst to work with Jim Nantz. This should not have come as a total surprise, given that Tony had spent time on television, had acted in a movie (*Trainwreck*), and had filmed commercials. He had all this experience in front of the camera in addition to his many years as the starter for the Cowboys. He replaced another former quarterback, Phil Simms, in the post with CBS.[34] He finished his career with the following statistics: a 78–49 mark as a starter, 2,829 completions in 4,335 attempts (a 65.3 percent rate), 248 touchdowns, 117 interceptions, and a 2–4 mark in the playoffs. As he set off to begin his work in the broadcast booth, just as had happened at EIU and Dallas, there were those who doubted him. Why did he get the lead assignment? How would he do in this difficult job? Well, it appeared that Tony would have to prove himself yet again.[35]

CONCLUSION

BROADCASTING CAREER AND WHY TONY ROMO'S STORY MATTERS, 2017–2021

any people were surprised when Tony signed to work with CBS to broadcast NFL games in April 2017, much less the fact that he became part of the number one team with Jim Nantz. Romo replaced not only a great, and Super Bowl–winning, quarterback, but also a man who had served in that role for 10 years: Phil Simms. Not all were pleased with the decision. For example, Jim Gorant at *Sports Illustrated* stated there were simply too many former Cowboys on the airwaves broadcasting the NFL. Among those individuals were Troy Aikman, Michael Irvin, former coach Jimmy Johnson, and others. This writer noted the appeal of the Cowboys, not only in Texas but nationwide, as one of the reasons for the presence of so many such ex-players/coaches on television. But he decided that the hiring of Romo was one too many. Of course, Gorant could not resist taking a shot at the newbie. "It's probably too cruel to say 'break a leg' to Romo. . . . But if CBS had asked if I wanted another Cowboy on TV, I would have stared into the distance and spit a wad of chaw. Tony Romo finally found a way to

remain working through the playoffs—he took a job as an analyst with CBS."[1] Another writer, Phil Mushnick, in a piece praising Simms' work, felt that he would have hired Romo: "he's engaging . . . often funny." But "would I have made him the No. 1 guy from Day 1? Not a chance."[2] As we have seen, in the past, others doubted whether Tony could do the job. He would certainly carry the same drive that he displayed as a Demon, Panther, and Cowboy into this new line of work.

Obviously, the folks at CBS were happy to have Tony on board. CBS Sports' chairman Sean McManus praised Tony and believed he would be a valuable addition. Romo, he noted, "will bring the same passion, enthusiasm, and knowledge that he displayed on the field. . . . He brings a fresh and insightful perspective to our viewers having just stepped off the field." Of course, the fact that Tony had done the television, commercial, and even movie work mentioned in the last chapter was part of the reason for his hiring. Additionally, as we have noted earlier, from the time he was in high school, many had noted his ability to read and unravel the intricacies of the sports he played.[3]

Before taking to the booth, Tony took time to work on another important part of his life: playing golf. About one month after retiring, he played in the local qualifying tournament for the U.S. Open. Although he fell short of his goal, he impressed his playing partner, David Lutterus, who had played in 48 Professional Golfers' Association events. "If he wanted to [become a pro] there's no question about it—I think he could make it.'" Lutterus then described how Tony handled a difficult hole and noted what that meant about how he read the golf course (like he "read" the court or the football field). The way he played that hole showed, "That's the way you've got to think. . . .

That's how the best think." After finishing his round, Tony compared playing golf to his new job. "I understand I'm coming in without any experience in that world . . . it's a little nerve-wracking. . . . That's why you love to do things."[4] Another key moment in Tony's life took place just before the start of his first broadcast when Candice gave birth to the couple's third son, Jones McCoy, in late August.

Well, given all the buildup, how did he do on his first broadcast? The reaction was quite positive. The upbeat comments came not just from fans but also from individuals who worked in broadcasting. For example, ESPN writer Bill Barnwell stated that Tony predicted things such as "calling out safety blitzes and pointing out that the Raiders ran on third down to go for it on fourth down." Rich Eisen of the NFL Network praised Romo as "excellent, knowledgeable, concise, likeable." Finally, Joon Lee of *Bleacher Report* noted that he "is really, really good at this . . . informative and he's already predicted a few play calls today. Lots of energy." Not a bad way to start a second career, right? One of the Cowboys' broadcasters, Brad Sham, was not surprised by Tony's success, as he contended that Tony had a great personality and only needed to get used to the technical things behind the scenes to shine in the booth. The writer of this story, Stefan Stevenson, asserted that "Romo's ease in the booth, his ability to clearly explain the intricacies of the game and his penchant for accurately predicting the upcoming play has created substantial excitement around his new career."[5]

The Stevenson article, published on November 3, came just a few days before a major (early) moment in Tony's broadcast career: when he would return to Texas to broadcast a Cowboys' home game for the first time. How would the fans react? Unlike so many times when Dallas came up short during his playing days, Sunday, November 5 was a perfect day. The team honored Romo before the game; fans clapped and cheered and held up "Thank you 9" signs for their former quarterback. Tony was touched by the love he felt from the crowd. "I wasn't prepared for that," he said. Then, as if the Cowboys had just received the opening kickoff of a game, Tony became a pro and did his duty. "He was prepared for his job . . . and quickly flashed the insight, humor and love for the game that has drawn him so much praise." On top of that, Dallas beat Kansas City, 28–17, as Dak Prescott threw for 249 yards and two scores on 21 of 33 attempts. Tony returned one more time to Dallas for a Thanksgiving Day game versus the Chargers. This time the Cowboys lost, 28–6.[6]

One thing that fans and others around the NFL took note of was the fact that, as an analyst, Tony got to broadcast the AFC Championship Game in early 2018. Many did not fail to mention that he never got this far during his playing days. Of course, he was asked if he missed playing and whether he was sorry that he never got to this point. Tony was very expressive in his response. Of course, he noted, he missed the game, and hoped that he could have led Dallas further, but now, "I know I didn't miss waking up on Mondays, taking your time getting out of bed. That was a little easier when the kids run and jump on your bed, get yourself up and going."[7]

After his first successful season behind a mike, Tony took time again for golf. In March 2018 he played a PGA tour event in the Dominican Republic, paired with legendary golfer John Daly. Later that spring, he once again tried to qualify for the U.S. Open but came up short.[8]

In late January 2019, Tony Romo finally got to the Super Bowl—to broadcast the game, that is. By this point in his new work, he had a reputation as a person who knew the game inside and out. He was so psychic that he had earned the nickname of "Romo-stradamus," a play on the name of Nostradamus, the famous sixteenth-century French mystic. At the media day before Super Bowl LIII (that number means 53), Tony was asked about the game as well as whether he would consider the chance of returning to Dallas, this time as a coach, as the team's offensive coordinator. "I'm sure one day I'll coach. Just right now, I'm happy with where I'm at. . . . I have three young boys at home that I want to be around and watch them grow up." Then, he was asked if he had mixed feelings about broadcasting the "big game" instead of playing in it. "It is one of my biggest disappointments. I wasn't able to do that. You leave your body, your heart and everything into it and you try. It's something you have to live with." On February 3, 2019, the Patriots and Tom Brady (of course) defeated the Los Angeles Rams, 13–3.[9]

After another positive season in the booth during the 2019 NFL campaign, other networks were interested in pursuing Tony to get him to leave CBS. However, he signed an extension in early 2020 to work for the network for up to 10 more years. The contract was worth a projected $180 million.[10]

The year 2020 also brought two other positive moments to Tony's life. First, his hometown of Burlington proposed to name the field at Don Dalton Stadium after him. Even with all the honors he earned at EIU and the NFL, this was a very special recognition. As you have seen, throughout his career, he remained tied to his hometown. There can be few tributes more important to an individual than to have the respect of the people you grew up with. While this was proposed in early 2020, as of May 2021, according to Peter Jackel, this had not yet been done. As for EIU, Romo's results with the Panthers also earned him a nomination, in June, to the College Football Hall of Fame for the 2021 class. The decision as to who would be inducted would take place early in the new year, and in January 2021, Tony got the call.[11]

Now that Tony has been inducted into the College Football Hall of Fame, many Cowboy fans are asking the next logical question: is he worthy to go into Canton, the Professional Football Hall of Fame? Well, that is tough to answer. Ty Schalter of FiveThirtyEight (https://fivethirty-eight.com) was one of the first to take on this possibility. In an article, the writer compared Romo to other great quarterbacks of the same era such as Peyton Manning, Drew Brees, Ben Roethlisberger, Philip Rivers, Aaron Rodgers, and others. Plenty of these players had passed for more yards (Manning, for example, passed for around 72,000), and all except Rivers had rings. While Tony's passing efficiency rating of 97.2 trails only Rodgers and Brady, Schalter argues that the lack of a Super Bowl win, plus the fact that he missed so much time due to injuries, makes Romo's case for induction into this grander hall of fame uncertain. As he summed up, "he was never quite the best . . . [and] his passing totals are perilously low to make the Hall of Fame. Unless voters go deep into what Romo did on the field and look past how many years he wasn't on it, he may be remembered as good, but not great." We will simply have to wait and see how things work out in regard to this honor.[12]

Along with all the good that happened for Tony Romo in 2020, there was a very sad moment in late October, as his beloved *abuelo*, Ramiro Sr., died at an assisted living facility in Burlington at the age of 87. As we have noted in this work, he was a man of great dignity and love for his fellow man. He served as a translator for Spanish speakers and broadcast religious programs in Spanish, and he and Feli served as marriage counselors to members of their church. Additionally, he became a deacon in the Catholic Church, a long and involved process. He had earned his pilot's license and loved to cook, especially enchiladas. At the time of his death, he and Feli had been married for 65 years. In his last days, one of the nurses who took care of him was his granddaughter, Tony's sister, Jossalyn Pennington. While it is always sad to say goodbye, the journey that Ramiro Sr. started truly revealed the best of the American Dream. He came from Mexico, worked hard, raised his family, and provided to his son, and later his grandchildren, opportunities that changed their clan and community for the better.[13]

So, how to sum up the life and careers of Tony Romo to this point? Well, it is certainly true that he is a role model for those who see themselves as underdogs. He was always a great athlete, but coming from a small town, it was easy to overlook him. He is also a wonderful example to persons of Latino descent. His family roots on his father's side come from Mexico—not exactly the first place one thinks of for a football player (of American football, that is). His grandfather and grandmother trekked to a place not usually associated with Mexicans or Mexican Americans— Wisconsin—yet there they built a rich life through their work and their community service, and by raising a wonderful family that nurtured the next generation: that of Tony and his sisters. No one expected much from a player from EIU, yet Romo surpassed quarterbacks with much more notable collegiate bloodlines. He started out very well, but then faced hardships, both mental and physical;

however, he continued to work hard and always gave his best. He faced adversity head on and did not flinch when the going got tough. After leaving the field, he took on a whole new career, one in which many doubted he would succeed. But there he triumphed again. He also continues to talk about his faith, to stage his camp in Burlington, and to contribute his time and money to many important charitable causes.

In July 2020, Joe Kozlowski, writing for sportscasting. com, neatly summarized the totality of not only Tony's experience but that of the Romo clan. "If all you only knew [of] Tony Romo [was] from his professional career, it might seem like he was born with a silver spoon in his mouth. For the quarterback's family, however, his success is the culmination of their American Dream."[14]

GLOSSARY

AFC: American Football Conference. One of two conferences that make up the **NFL**. At the end of the season, the team that wins this conference plays against the **NFC** champion in the Super Bowl.

At-large bids: The **NCAA** awards an opportunity for several teams to enter the small school playoffs if they do not win their conference titles.

Audibles: When a quarterback, after assigning a play in the huddle, determines that the defense is well prepared for the play and changes the play to one more suitable against the defense before the snap of the ball.

Blitz/Bull rush: When defensive players other than those on the defensive line rush to try to tackle the quarterback. There are various types of blitzes. Sometimes, it will be the linebackers who blitz; other times, it will be a player from the secondary (such as a cornerback or safety).

Bootleg: When a quarterback, after taking the snap, does not drop straight back but rather rolls out to either the left or the right in order to avoid the rush of the defense.

Check-off passes: When the quarterback, seeing receivers farther down field are covered, throws a short pass to a receiver closer to him (this is often to a running back).

Cut: When a team decides that they do not want to keep a player on their roster.

Free agent: A player who is signed by a team but who was not selected during the draft.

Interception/Pick: This occurs when the quarterback launches a pass toward a receiver, but the pass is caught by a defensive player instead.

Major leagues: The highest level of professional baseball.

Minicamps: Practices held by teams shortly after the draft. The players who attend are those who were selected in the draft and the **free agents**. **NFL** teams will have a second minicamp that is also attended by veterans.

NBA: National Basketball Association—the highest level of professional basketball.

NCAA: National Collegiate Athletic Association—the organization that determines the rules and regulations for collegiate sports.

NFC: National Football Conference—one of two conferences that make up the National Football League (**NFL**). At the end of the season, the team that wins this conference plays against the **AFC** champion in the Super Bowl.

NFL: The highest level of professional football.

NFL Europe: A league sponsored by the **NFL** that featured teams in Europe and that was designed to provide extra practice games for players on NFL teams. The league existed from 1991 to 2007.

No-huddle offense: Instead of going into a huddle and calling the play, the quarterback will call the plays on the line of scrimmage in order to use as little time as possible. Usually used when a team is behind and needs to save time as they drive down the field.

Passing efficiency: A complex formula that is used to determine how effective a quarterback is. It focuses (among other things) on completion percentage, touchdowns, and interceptions thrown.

Pocket: When a quarterback drops back to pass, the offensive line tries to create space so that he can throw the ball with a clear line of sight. The goal is to keep defensive players outside of this area to make it easier for the quarterback to read what is going on downfield.

Practice squad: Players who are still attached to an **NFL** club but who do not dress for games. If a player at a certain position gets hurt, the team may "call up" a practice squad player and "dress" him for games.

Pro Bowl: The All-Star game of the **NFL**.

Progressions: As various receivers run downfield, the quarterback knows where each of them is supposed to be. The quarterback has a primary receiver, which is the first place he would like to throw the ball. If that player is covered, then the quarterback moves his sight to the second receiver, and so forth. At the high school level, most quarterbacks will have only two progressions. At the collegiate and professional levels, there are more progressions. All of this happens within a few seconds. In the **NFL**, most quarterbacks have to throw the ball within three seconds.

"Reading" the field: When a quarterback looks at the defense across the line of scrimmage and determines whether the play called in the huddle is likely to succeed. If he believes that it will not be effective against the way the defense is lined up, he will call an **audible**.

Redshirt: College players have four years of eligibility to play for a university. By redshirting, a player is allowed to participate in some activities but does not use up a year of his four years of eligibility. Usually, the redshirt year is when a player is a freshman.

Sack: This occurs when a defender tackles the quarterback behind the line of scrimmage.

Short field: This occurs when a team turns the ball over to the opponent's offense on their side of the field. This can happen because of a turnover or a returned kick.

Special teams: This is the third part of a football team. You have the offense, the goal of which is to score. You have the defense, the goal of which is to keep the other team from scoring. The special teams are involved in kickoffs and punts.

Spring scrimmage: A game that takes place at the end of a football camp. A given team (**NFL**, college, or high school) is divided up, and the squads usually are named after one of the two team colors. So, for the EIU Panthers, it was White and Blue. This is designed to simulate a regular game.

Stoop labor: Agricultural labor performed in a stooping or squatting position—for example, hoeing beets with a short hoe. The type of work that many Mexicans and Mexican Americans did in Wisconsin.

Super Bowl: The **NFL**'s championship game contested between the winner of the **AFC** and the **NFC**.

Three and out: This occurs when an offensive team is unable to gain the required number of yards (10) in order to keep possession of the football. If the offense does not generate the needed yardage in three plays, they have to turn the ball over to the other team.

Walter Payton Award: Named in honor of the late Walter Payton, who played at a small school (Jackson State University) but went on to be one of the greatest running backs in the history of the **NFL**. This award is the small school equivalent of the Heisman Trophy, which is given to the best player in Division I football.

NOTES

CHAPTER 1

1. https://www.britannica.com/place/Muzquiz.

2. Jason Bunch, "Coahuila's Historic Ties to San Antonio," *San Antonio Express-News*, August 2, 2014.

3. Roberto M. Sanchez, "Proud Grandparents Get Taste of Romomania," *Dallas Morning News*, December 25, 2006, https://www.pressreader.com/usa/the-dallas-morning-news/20061225/281900178725786.

4. This information comes from a 1950 report to the governor of Wisconsin. See Wisconsin Governor's Commission on Human Rights, "Migratory Agricultural Workers in Wisconsin: A Problem in Human Rights" (Madison, WI: Governor's Commission on Human Rights, June 1950), https://content.wisconsinhistory.org/digital/collection/tp/id/57316.

5. David Flores, "Football: Romo's Grandparents Revel in His First Game as Cowboys' Starter," *San Antonio Express-News*, November 1, 2006, https://web.archive.org/web/20061110190340/http://www.mysanantonio.com/sports/football/nfl/cowboys/stories/MYSA110306.01D.FBNcowboys.romo.2c1062c.html.

6. Elizabeth Brandeis Raushenbush, *The Migrant Labor Problem in Wisconsin* (Madison, WI: Governor's Commission on Human Rights, 1962), https://content.wisconsinhistory.org/digital/collection/tp/id/50059https://content.wisconsinhistory.org/digital/

collection/tp/id/50031.

7.   Victoria Hirschberg, "Wisconsin," in *Latino America: A State-by-State Encyclopedia*, ed. Mark Overmeyer-Velazquez (Westport, CT: Greenwood Press, 2008), 867–82.

8.   "Los Abuelos de Tony Romo," January 10, 2008, https://www.youtube.com/watch?v=qB2RgYLJ3N8.

9.   S. L. Price, "Why Ya Gotta Hate? Inside Romo's Rise From Obscurity to Brightest Spotlight," *Sports Illustrated*, October 15, 2014, https://www.si.com/nfl/2014/10/15/tony-romo-dallas-cowboys#.

10.   Sandra Velazquez, "Abuelos de Tony Romo quieren compartir su fe y los valores familiares," *Hoy Dallas*, April 29, 2017, https://www.hoydallas.com/hoy-dfw/metroplex/3013-abuelos-de-tony-romo-quieren-compartir-su-fe-y-los-valores-familiares.html.

11.   Roberto M. Sanchez, "Proud Grandparents Get Taste of Romomania," *Dallas Morning News*, December 25, 2006.

12.   Diane Collins, "Romo, 50th 6-25-05," *The Journal Times*, June 25, 2005, https://journaltimes.com/news/local/romo-th/article_0da64065-6538-5ec4-a318-922af-a21bde5.html.

13.   Peter Jackel, "Romo Stays True to His Roots," *The Journal Times*, June 23, 2008, https://journal-times.com/sports/jackel-romo-stays-true-to-roots/article_a8a8a08e-4e35-5952-a7fb-31e69feeb70e.html.

14.   Mac Engel, *Tony Romo: America's Next Quarterback* (Chicago, IL: Triumph Books, 2007), 27.

15.   For a history of the city of Burlington, see https://www.wisconsinhistory.org/Records/Article/CS2403.

16.   Peter Jackel, "Romo Stays True to His Roots," *The Journal Times*, June 23, 2008.

CHAPTER 2

1. Tom Mackin, "Senior Romo Takes Turn in the Spotlight," *USGA*, September 25, 2015, https://www.usga.org/championships/2015/u-s--senior-amateur-/articles/senior-romo-takes-turn-in-spotlight.html. See also Mac Engel, *Tony Romo: America's Next Quarterback*, 29.

2. Graham Bensinger, "My Dad Made $500 Per Month," March 26, 2020, https://www.youtube.com/watch?v=n4MmfQhyhyU.

3. Peter Simek, "Tony Romo: The Natural," *D Magazine*, September 2012, https://www.dmagazine.com/publications/d-magazine/2012/september/tony-romo-the-natural/.

4. "History of Little League Baseball in Burlington," https://burlingtonhistory.org/history-little-league-baseball-burlington.

5. Mac Engel, *Tony Romo: America's Next Quarterback*, 29.

6. "Burlington Middle," *The Journal Times*, July 2, 1994, 33.

7. Mac Engel, *Tony Romo: America's Next Quarterback*, 29.

8. "Local: Racine County Junior Tournament," *The Journal Times*, July 8, 1994, 26.

9. "Like Fathers, Like Sons," *The Journal Times*, May 26, 1995, 34.

10. Jeffrey Stern, "SLC Takes on a Whole New Look," *The Journal Times*, November 24, 1995, 31.

11. Peter Jackel, "Tipping the Scales His Way," *The Journal Times*, April 7, 1996, 8B.

12. Robb Luehr, "Laehr Weathered Storm," *The Journal Times*, June 20, 1996, 31.

13. Mac Engel, *Tony Romo: America's Next Quarterback*, 29.

14. Ibid., 25.

15. Ibid., 31. See also S. L. Price, "Why Ya Gotta Hate?

Inside Romo's Rise from Obscurity to Brightest Spotlight," *Sports Illustrated*, December 2, 2013, https://vault.si.com/vault/2013/12/02/why-ya-gotta-hate.

16. Jon Coca, "Burlington's Romo Lets Actions Do the Talking on Court and Field," *The Journal Times*, December 19, 1996, 31.

17. Peter Jackel, "Radl's Dedication Pays Off," *The Journal Times*, April 15, 1997, 22.

18. Robb Luehr, "Representin'," *The Journal Times*, March 19, 1998, 32, and *Fond Du Lac Commonwealth Reporter*, March 25, 1998, 27.

19. S. L. Price, "Why Ya Gotta Hate?"

20. Peter Simek, "Tony Romo: The Natural."

21. Peter Jackel, "Football: Burlington, Romo Had a Season to Remember in 1996," *The Journal Times*, May 5, 2020, https://journaltimes.com/sports/football/football-burlington-romo-had-season-to-remember-in-1996/article_ba6cadcf-aea3-5c3c-be12-f8b00a7f868b.html.

22. Peter Simek, "Tony Romo: The Natural."

23. Peter Jackel, "Football: Burlington, Romo Had a Season to Remember in 1996."

24. Robb Luehr, "Prep Notebook," *The Journal Times*, September 13, 1996, 33.

25. Peter Jackel, "A Look at Racine County's Top Players," *The Journal Times*, November 29, 1996, 34.

26. Mac Engel, *Tony Romo: America's Next Quarterback*, 33.

27. Peter Simek, "Tony Romo: The Natural." See also "Athletes of the Week," *The Journal Times*, October 2, 1997, 29.

28. Peter Simek, "Tony Romo: The Natural." See also Peter Jackel, "It's Last Call for Burlington's Quarterback," *The Journal Times*, October 21, and "Solitary Man," *The*

Journal Times, December 7, 1997, 17.

29.   See Peter Simek, "Tony Romo: The Natural," and Mac
        Engel, *Tony Romo: America's Next Quarterback*, 35.

CHAPTER 3

1.   *EIU Football History*, https://eiu_ftp.sidearmsports.
        com/custompages/Record_Books/Football%20
        Record%20 Book.pdf.

2.   Ibid.

3.   Brian Nielsen, "EIU Lands Two Prep Quarterbacks," and
        "Eastern Signs Big Class," *Journal Gazette*, January 31,
        1998, 9 and 14; and February 5, 1998, 9.

4.   Brian Nielsen, "EIU Settles on Odam to Open," and
        "Panthers' Buich Ahead of His Class," *Journal Gazette*,
        August 24, 1998, 11; and December 18, 1998, 19.

5.   Gery Woelfel, "Bonus Shots," *The Journal Times*,
        November 18, 1998, 12.

6.   Mac Engel, *Tony Romo: America's Next Quarterback*, 37.

7.   Brian Nielsen, "Spring Football Draws Spoo's Review,"
        and "Opener Near for Eastern," *Journal Gazette*, August
        27, 1999, 13; and August 31, 1999, 11. See also *EIU
        Football History*, 49.

8.   Brian Nielsen, "Panthers Notch First Win," *Journal
        Gazette*, September 27, 1999, 11.

9.   Brian Nielsen, "Buich Doubtful for Central Florida,"
        and "Eastern Looking for a Way to Knock Off Central
        Florida," *Journal Gazette*, September 30, 1999, 11; and
        October 2, 1999, 18.

10.   "Eastern Plays Better in Loss to Central Florida," *Journal
        Gazette*, October 4, 1999, 11.

11.   Brian Nielsen, "Late Score Not Needed for Talented
        Tigers," and "Tennessee State Overpowers EIU," *Journal
        Gazette*, October 11, 1999, 15.

12. Peter Jackel, "Romo Passes His Early College Exam," *The Journal Times*, October 22, 1999, 31.

13. Brian Nielsen, "Jordan Appears to Be on Way to EIU," *Journal Gazette*, December 18, 1999, 15.

14. Brian Nielsen, "A Busy Recruiting Day for EIU"; "Spring Practice Monday for EIU Football"; "Panthers Adjusting to Change"; and "EIU Football Draft is Today," *Journal Gazette*, February 3, 2000, 11; March 31, 2000, 14; April 12, 2000, 13; and April 27, 2000, 14.

15. Brian Nielsen, "Eastern Glad to Have Two QB Candidates," *Journal Gazette*, August 9, 2000, 11.

16. Brian Nielsen, "Romo Does Well in EIU Scrimmage," and "New Years, New QBs, New Hope for Eastern," *Journal Gazette*, August 21, 2000, 16; and August 31, 2000, 11.

17. Brian Nielsen, "Eastern Wins Convincingly"; "Division II School No Pushover"; "EIU Rolls to 72–0 Win Over Kentucky Wesleyan"; "Eastern Offense to be Tested"; and "Eastern Comes Up Just Short," *Journal Gazette*, September 1, 2000, 11; September 9, 2000, 16; September 11, 2000, 11; September 14, 2000, 14; and September 18, 2000, 1. See also "Romo is OVC Player of Week," *Journal Gazette*, September 5, 2000, 16.

18. Brian Nielsen, "Panthers' Goal is Not to Overlook UT–Martin"; "Eastern Taking UT–Martin Seriously"; "Panthers Return to Win Column"; "After Bye Week Come Tough Tests"; "Romo Tops in Passing Efficiency"; "Panthers Aim for Homecoming Win"; "Eastern Rallies to Top Tennessee State"; and "Panthers Crack Top 25," *Journal Gazette*, September 21, 2000, 11; September 23, 2000, 16; September 25, 2000, 11; September 28, 2000, 11; October 4, 2000, 14; October 7, 2000, 11; October 9, 2000, 11; and October 10, 2000, 13.

19. Brian Nielsen, "Romo's Six TD Passes Lead Eastern"; Tennessee Tech Tries to Stop Eastern"; and "Panthers Continue Winning Streak," *Journal Gazette*, October 16, 2000; October 21, 2000; and October 23, 2000, 11.

20. See also "Eastern Now in Both I-AA Polls," *Journal Gazette*, October 17, 2000, 14.

21. Brian Nielsen, "Strong Western Kentucky Team Throttles Eastern," *Journal Gazette*, October 30, 2000, 11.

22. Brian Nielsen, "Panthers Put Away SEMO, 38–9"; "EIU Prepares for Surging ISU"; "Eastern Drops Thriller to ISU"; "Last Chance for EIU"; and "Panthers Roar to Easy Victory," *Journal Gazette*, November 6, 2000; November 9, 2000, 11; November 13, 2000; November 18, 2000, 11; and November 20, 2000, 11.

23. Brian Nielsen, "Grizzlies Put End to EIU Season," *Journal Gazette*, November 27, 2000, 10.

24. Brian Nielsen, "Spoo Second in Eddie Robinson Voting," *Journal Gazette*, December 6, 2000, 11. See also "Young, Romo Earn Honorable Mention All-American Honors," *Journal Gazette*, January 24, 2001, 11.

CHAPTER 4

1. Brian Nielsen, "Some Uncertainty as EIU Enters Spring," *Journal Gazette*, March 31, 2001, 16.

2. Ibid.

3. Brian Nielsen, "Romo Hungry for Successful Season," *Journal Gazette*, August 8, 2001, 14.

4. Ibid.

5. Brian Nielsen, "College Football News You Can Use While Waiting," September 1, 2001, 19.

6. Brian Nielsen, "Eastern Impressive in 44–14 Win Over Indiana State"; "Spoo: As Big of a Road Win as We've Had"; "Stressful Week Has Happy End for Cutolo";

"Panthers Play Sloppy, Beat Tennessee Tech"; "Eastern Now No. in I-AA"; and "Versatility, Efficiency in EIU's Favor Against I-A Aztecs," *Journal Gazette*, September 10, 2001, 11; September 24, 2001, 13 and 16; September 24, 2001, 13 and 16; October 1, 2001, 11; October 2, 2001, 14; and October 6, 2001, 14.

7.   Brian Nielsen, "Ned Runs San Diego State Past Eastern," *Journal Gazette*, October 8, 2001, 15.

8.   Brian Nielsen, "No-Passing Panthers Run Past SEMO"; "No Let Down as Panthers Pound SIU"; "Win for First is One for the Ages"; "Panthers Blow Past Tennessee–Martin"; "Win Comes with a Price for Panthers"; and "Ohio Valley Champions," *Journal Gazette*, October 15, 2001, 13; October 22, 2001, 11; October 29, 2001, 11; November 2, 2001, 11; November 12, 2001, 14; and November 19, 2001, 11.

9.   Brian Nielsen, "Panthers Get Northern Iowa at Home"; "Romo is OVC Player of the Year Again"; and "Romo, Ricks Take Top OVC Football Honors," *Journal Gazette*, November 26, 2001, 11; November 27, 2001, 11; and November 27, 2001, 11.

10.   Brian Nielsen, "Special Teams Haunt Eastern in Loss to UNI"; and "Comeback Falls Short, Playoff Year Ends," *Journal Gazette*, December 3, 2001, 16; December 3, 2001, 14. See also "Romo, Ricks Gain AP All-American Third-Team Honors," *Journal Gazette*, December 19, 2001, 16.

11.   Brian Nielsen, "Panthers Set to Spring into Action" and "Panthers No. 4 in Preseason Poll," *Journal Gazette*, March 25, 2002, 13 and August 13, 2002, 11. See also "Magazine Tabs Romo as I-AA Player of Year" and "More Recognition for Romo, Ricks and EIU," *Journal Gazette*, July 5, 2002, 11 and July 10, 2002, 11.

12. Brian Nielsen, "Big Plays Lead to Panther Loss"; "'We're Stepping Out of Our League,' Spoo Says"; and "'Funny' Start Winds Up a K-State Laugher," *Journal Gazette*, September 3, 2002, 14; September 12, 2002, 13; and September 16, 2002, 13.

13. Brian Nielsen, "What an Incredible Finish," *Journal Gazette*, October 14, 2002, 14.

14. Bill Jauss, "Romo Takes Aim at NFL," *Chicago Tribune*, October 18, 2002, 4.

15. Mike Monahan, "Eastern Clinches OVC Title," *Journal Gazette*, November 11, 2002, 11.

16. Brian Nielsen, "Taylor, Romo Set Records in EIU Win"; and "Eastern Loses to Murray on Last-Second Field Goal," *Journal Gazette*, November 18, 2002, 15 and November 25, 2002, 15.

17. "Romo, Ricks Take Top OVC Football Honors," *Journal Gazette*, November 27, 2002, 14.

18. *EIU Football History*, 16 and 17.

19. Brian Nielsen, "Western's Rush-Hour D Stalls EIU in Playoff Trip," *Journal Gazette*, December 2, 2002, 13.

20. Brian Nielsen, "Romo One of Three Payton Finalists," *Journal Gazette*, December 4, 2002, 11.

21. Brian Nielsen, "Will Payton Voters Select Romo, Too?" *Journal Gazette*, December 19, 2002, 14.

22. Brian Nielsen, "EIU Quarterback Wins Payton Award," *Journal Gazette*, December 20, 2002, 13.

CHAPTER 5

1. "Romo Wins 2002 Walter Payton Award," *EIU Football History*, 5.

2. Brian Nielsen, "EIU Quarterback Romo Ready for NFL Combine," *Journal Gazette*, January 9, 2003, 14.

3. "Romo Throws 2 TDs in All-Star Game," *Journal*

Gazette, January 27, 2003, 16.

4. Brian Nielsen, "Improved Romo Has Impressive Combine," *Journal Gazette*, February 24, 2003, 13.

5. Robb Luehr, "Romo Receives Hero's Welcome," *The Journal Times*, March 5, 2003, 35.

6. Peter Jackel, "Good Impression: Romo Solidifies His Draft Position at NFL Combine," *The Journal Times*, March 10, 2003, 21 and 22.

7. "Prospect Profiles: Tony Romo," *Internet Archive: Wayback Machine*, https://web.archive.org/web/20030625064653/http://www.nfl.com/draft/profiles/romo_tony.

8. Peter Jackel, "Hearing the Call," *The Journal Times*, April 24, 2003, 33 and 35.

9. Peter Jackel, "Cowboys Come Callin'," *The Journal Times*, April 28, 2003, 21 and 24. See also Brian Nielsen, "Cowboys Corral Romo," *Decatur Herald & Review*, April 29, 2003, 13.

10. "2002 Dallas Cowboys Statistics & Players," https://www.pro-football-reference.com/teams/dal/2002.htm.

11. Jennifer Floyd, "Quarterback Job Up for Grabs," and "Did You Hear the One About the QBs?" *Fort Worth Star-Telegram*, May 3, 2003, 59 and May 4, 2003, 81.

12. Peter Jackel, "Romo Holds His Own," *The Journal Times*, May 6, 2003, 25.

13. MIT is the Massachusetts Institute of Technology, a highly prestigious university. See the following: Jennifer Floyd, "Parcells Tepid on Other QB Options," *Fort Worth Star-Telegram*, May 20, 2003, 3D; Clarissa Aljentera, "Making Roster Can Be Big Stretch for Some," *Fort Worth Star-Telegram*, May 28, 2003, 6D; Jennifer Floyd, "Stars on Helmets Only," *Fort Worth Star-Telegram*, June 8, 2003, 11C; and Peter Jackel, "Romo Raises Stakes," *The Journal Times*, June 11, 2003.

14. Dan Benton, "20 Greatest Undrafted Free Agents in NFL History," *Touchdown Wire, USA Today*, March 23, 2019, https://touchdownwire.usatoday.com/2019/03/2 3/20-greatest-undrafted-free-agents-nfl-history/5/.

15. Brian Nielsen, "So Far, So Good for Tony Romo," *Journal Gazette*, August 6, 2003, 9; Peter Jackel, "Romo Moving Up Dallas' Depth Chart," *The Journal Times*, August 8, 2003, 27; and Charles Polansky, "Rookie Center Undergoes Knee Surgery," *Fort Worth Star-Telegram*, August 8, 2003, 14D.

16. Peter Jackel, "Romo Feels a Big Blast of Hot Air," *The Journal Times*, August 11, 2003, 21; "Making the Grade," *The Journal Times*, August 17, 2003, 17; and "Romo Earns his NFL Spurs," *The Journal Times*, September 1, 2003, 35.

17. "2003 Dallas Cowboys, Statistics and Players," https:// www.pro-football-reference.com/teams/dal/2003.htm.

18. Brian Nielsen, "Romo Adding to His Own Legend," *Journal Gazette*, October 25, 2003, 14.

19. Peter Jackel, "Football Turns Out to Be the Right Fit for Romo After All," *The Journal Times*, November 13, 2003, 48.

20. "Grading the Offense," *Fort Worth Star-Telegram*, December 31, 2003, 6D.

21. Mac Engel, *Tony Romo: America's Next Quarterback*, 67 and 70.

22. Brian Nielsen, "Romo Not Buying Practice Squad Talk," *Decatur Herald-Review*, July 29, 2004, 14.

23. Brian Nielsen, "Cowboys Shockingly Release QB Carter," *Journal Gazette*, August 5, 2004, 9. See also Jim Reeves, "Cowboys Shoulda, Coulda in Off-Season," *Fort Worth Star-Telegram*, August 8, 2004, 4C; and Jennifer Floyd Engel, "Cowboys Not Giving Up at QB," *Fort*

Worth Star-Telegram, August 17, 2004, 10D.

24. Jennifer Floyd Engel, "The 'Boys are Back and Inexperienced," *Fort Worth Star-Telegram*, August 22, 2004, 4C; and Clarence E. Hill Jr., "Cowboys Inch Ahead in Close Win Over Raiders," *Fort Worth Star-Telegram*, August 22, 2004, 4C.

25. Jennifer Floyd Engel, "Romo Makes Strong Case to be Vinny's Backup," *Fort Worth Star-Telegram*, September 3, 2004, 10D; Mac Engel, "Secondary Changes Will Be Problematic," *Fort Worth Star-Telegram*, September 13, 2004, 6DD; and Clarence E. Hill Jr., "George Still Looking to Solidify Role on Offense," *Fort Worth Star-Telegram*, September 25, 2004, 7D.

26. Jennifer Floyd Engel, "Romo Stays Ahead of Henson For Now," *Fort Worth Star-Telegram*, October 2, 2004, 6D.

27. Jennifer Floyd Engel, "Is the Future Now?"; "Ready or Not, Henson is Likely to Start Today"; and "No Closer to a Quarterback Solution," *Fort Worth Star-Telegram*, November 9, 2004, 1D; November 25, 2004, 13D; and November 27, 2004, 1D. See also "2004 Dallas Cowboys Statistics and Players," https://www.pro-football-reference.com/teams/dal/2004.htm.

28. Gil LeBreton, "It's About Henson, Not Romo," *Fort Worth Star-Telegram*, December 17, 2004, 1D.

29. Rick Herrin, "Vinny Pondering Future," *Fort Worth Star-Telegram*, December 31, 2004, 5D; Jennifer Floyd Engel, "No Word Yet on Testaverde's Potential Return," *Fort Worth Star-Telegram*, January 5, 2005, 5D; "Jones Says He'll Stand Pat at QB," *Fort Worth Star-Telegram*, January 15, 2005, 1D; "Jones Says Cowboys Will Dive into Free-Agent Pool," *Fort Worth Star-Telegram*, February 18, 2005, 1D; and "Is 8 Enough," *Fort Worth*

Star-Telegram, February 24, 2005, 1D; Clarence E. Hill Jr., "Cowboys Won't Send Young QBs to Europe," *Fort Worth Star-Telegram*, January 22, 2005, 1D.

30. Clarence E. Hill, "Former Pro Bowler Squeezed Out by Cap," *Fort Worth Star-Telegram*, March 2, 2005, 10D; "Ex-Teammates Eager to Acquire Howard's Help," March 15, 2005, 3D; and "Romo Secures New Deal; Cowboys Look for Safety," May 21, 2005, 3D.

31. "2005 Dallas Cowboys Statistics and Players," https://www.pro-football-reference.com/teams/dal/2005.htm.

32. Jennifer Floyd Engel, "Backup Plan," *Fort Worth Star-Telegram*, August 13, 2005, 1C.

33. Randy Galloway, "Romo Has Earned Best Job in Football," *Fort Worth Star-Telegram*, August 19, 2005, 1D and 10D.

34. Jennifer Floyd Engel, "Jones Remains Supportive of Henson," *Fort Worth Star-Telegram*, August 30, 2005, 6D.

35. Gil LeBreton, "Cowboys' Romo Wasn't Built (Up) in a Day," *Fort Worth Star-Telegram*, August 29, 2005, 1D and 8D.

36. Jennifer Floyd Engel, "Backup Plan OK for Romo," *Fort Worth Star-Telegram*, September 4, 2005, 1C and 11C.

CHAPTER 6

1. Mac Engel, "Place Value: Bledsoe Certain Dallas Will Be His Last Stand," *Fort Worth Star-Telegram*, December 30, 2005, 1D.

2. Randy Galloway, "QB School," *Fort Worth Star-Telegram*, January 22, 2006, 1C; Jennifer Floyd Engel, "Cowboys Need to Stick with Bledsoe," *Fort Worth Star-Telegram*, February 27, 2006, D1 and D6; Mac Engel, "European Plan," *Fort Worth Star-Telegram*, March 10, 2006; 8D; and Gil LeBreton, "No Reaching, Hoping for Cowboys,"

Fort Worth Star-Telegram, April 21, 2006, 1D and 5D.

3.   Clarence E. Hill Jr., "Romo Faces Big Test," *Fort Worth Star-Telegram*, August 1, 2006, 8D, and Jim Reeves, "Cowboys Have No Backup Plan at QB," *Fort Worth Star-Telegram*, August 2, 2006, D1.

4.   Jennifer Floyd Engel, "Cowboys QB Plans Puzzling," *Fort Worth Star-Telegram*, August 12, 2006, D1; and Clarence E. Hill Jr., "Romo Passes the Test," *Fort Worth Star-Telegram*, August 13, 2006, 9C.

5.   Len Pasquarelli, "Sources: Johnson to Get Start for Vikings," *ESPN News*, December 6, 2006, https://www.espn.com/nfl/news/story?id=2688804.

6.   Jennifer Floyd Engel, "Let's Rethink T. O.'s Importance," *Fort Worth Star-Telegram*, August 27, 2006, 2C, and "Too Soon to Sell Out Bledsoe," August 17, 2006, 2D; Clarence E. Hill Jr., "Henson Loses Touch in Quarterback Race," *Fort Worth Star-Telegram*, August 17, 2006, 10D; and Mac Engel, "Bledsoe Totters; Romo Prepares," *Fort Worth Star-Telegram*, September 1, 2006, 8D.

7.   Clarence E. Hill Jr., "Same Song, New Verse," *Fort Worth Star-Telegram*, September 11, 2006, 4DD; Randy Galloway, "Bledsoe's Performance Will Only Fuel Talk of Controversy," *Fort Worth Star-Telegram*, September 11, 2006, 1DD and 5DD; and Gil LeBreton, "Parcells Prescribes 2nd Dose of Bledsoe," *Fort Worth Star-Telegram*, September 12, 2006, 1D and 3D.

8.   Jim Reeves, "Ready or Not, Here Comes Tony Romo," *Fort Worth Star-Telegram*, September 17, 2006, 6C.

9.   See https://www.pro-football-reference.com/teams/dal/2006.htm.

10.   "Quarter-by-Quarter Replay," *Fort Worth Star-Telegram*, October 24, 2006, A2.

11. Mac Engel, "Benching Miffs Bledsoe," *Fort Worth Star-Telegram*, October 24, 2006, 3DD; Randy Galloway, "Bledsoe Leaves Parcells No Choice But to Turn to Romo," *Fort Worth Star-Telegram*, October 24, 2006, 1DD and 4DD; Mac Engel, "Snap Decision," *Fort Worth Star-Telegram*, October 25, 2006, D1; and Clarence E. Hill Jr., "A Forward Pass: Parcells Turns to Romo for Present and, Maybe, Future," *Fort Worth Star-Telegram*, October 26, 2006, 1D and 5D.

12. "Owner Disappointed About Romo Promotion," *Decatur Herald and Review*, October 27, 2006, 14.

13. Clarence Hill Jr., "New Role, Same Swagger," *Fort Worth Star-Telegram*, October 29, 2006, 6C.

14. "Quarter-by-Quarter Replay," *Fort Worth Star-Telegram*, October 30, 2006, 4DD; Randy Galloway, "First Start Jitters Not a Factor for Romo," "Quarter-by-Quarter Replay," *Fort Worth Star-Telegram*, October 30, 2006, 1DD and 6DD; and Gil LeBreton, "Report of Boys' Demise Exaggerated," and "Quarter-by-Quarter Replay," *Fort Worth Star-Telegram*, October 30, 2006, 1DD, 4DD, and 5DD.

15. Mac Engel, "Romo's Play Off the Charts . . . So Far," *Fort Worth Star-Telegram*, October 31, 2006, 1D and 4D and Clarence E. Hill Jr., "Romo Stays on Even Keel," "Quarter-by-Quarter Replay," *Fort Worth Star-Telegram*, November 2, 2006, D1.

16. Jennifer Floyd Engel, "An All-In Situation for Romo," *Fort Worth Star-Telegram*, November 4, 2006, 2C.

17. Clarence E. Hill Jr., "Yet Another Roadblock," *Fort Worth Star-Telegram*, November 6, 2006, 4CC.

18. Rick Herrin, "Romo Has Put Life in the Offense," *Fort Worth Star-Telegram*, November 11, 2006, 1D and 7D.

19. Clarence E. Hill Jr., "Taking Care of Business," *Fort*

Worth Star-Telegram, November 13, 2006, 4DD; Jim Reeves, "Babe Was on the Money," *Fort Worth Star-Telegram*, November 19, 2006, 10C; and Jennifer Floyd Engel, "Gift of Romo Keeps Giving," *Fort Worth Star-Telegram*, November 19, 2006, 2C.

20. Clarence E. Hill Jr., "'Boys Look Like Real Deal," *Fort Worth Star-Telegram*, November 20, 2006, 4DD; and Jennifer Floyd Engel, "Romo's Star on the Rise," *Fort Worth Star-Telegram*, November 21, 2006, 2D.

21. Tim Layden, "Silver Star," *Sports Illustrated*, December 11, 2006, https://vault.si.com/vault/2006/12/11/silver-star. See also Mac Engel, *Tony Romo: America's Next Quarterback*, 94–95.

22. Clarence E. Hill Jr., "Cowboys Crash to Earth," *Fort Worth Star-Telegram*, December 11, 2006, 4DD.

23. Clarence E. Hill Jr., "A 'Character' Comeback," *Fort Worth Star-Telegram*, December 17, 2006, 4CC.

24. Mac Engel, *Tony Romo: America's Next Quarterback*, 97; and "Eagles' Pressure Has Romo on Run," *Fort Worth Star-Telegram*, December 26, 2006, 10DD.

25. Mac Engel, *Tony Romo: America's Next Quarterback*, 99; Rick Herrin, "World Crashing on Romo," *Fort Worth Star-Telegram*, January 1, 2007, 6DD; and Gil LeBreton, "Boo Birds Bring Romo Back to Earth," *Fort Worth Star-Telegram*, January 1, 2007, 1DD and 6DD.

26. Rick Herrin, "Cowboys' Romo a Confidence Man," *Fort Worth Star-Telegram*, January 3, 2007, 8D; and Randy Galloway, "Romo Still Cowboys' Biggest Hope," *Fort Worth Star-Telegram*, January 5, 2207, 1D and 4D.

27. Clarence E. Hill Jr., "A Season Fumbled Away," *Fort Worth Star-Telegram*, January 7, 2007, 4CC; and Charean Williams, "Not-so-Special Ending," *Fort Worth Star-Telegram*, January 7, 2007, 6CC.

28. Mac Engel, *Tony Romo: America's Next Quarterback*, 107.

29. Chris Mortensen, "Parcells Signs Four-Year Deal to Head Dolphins' Football Operations," *ESPN News*, December 20, 2007, https://www.espn.com/nfl/news/story?id=3162909.

30. Gil LeBreton, "Don't Abandon Ship; Play with Abandon," *Fort Worth Star-Telegram*, January 8, 2007, 1D; Randy Galloway, "A History Lesson for Romo," *Fort Worth Star-Telegram*, 11, 2007, 1D; "Five Questions the Cowboys Must Answer to Turn This Thing Around," *Fort Worth Star-Telegram*, January 11, 2007, 1D.

31. Greg Beacham, "Last-Second Kick Stymies NFC Rally," *Fort Worth Star-Telegram*, February 11, 2007, 17C.

CHAPTER 7

1. Mac Engel, "Raising a Star," *Fort Worth Star-Telegram*, January 6, 2007, 55–56.

2. David Flores, "David Flores: After 43-Plus Years, It's Time to Lay Down My Bucket and Move On," July 10, 2020, https://www.kens5.com/article/sports/david-flores-after-43-plus-years-its-time-to-lay-down-my-bucket-and-move-on/273-6bd15ca8-084e-41c1-a37e-622b8903c1ac.

3. David Flores, "Proud Grandparents," *The Journal Times*, December 3, 2006, 1.

4. Melissa Isaacson, "Rising Star Stays Grounded," *Chicago Tribune*, December 3, 2006, 7.

5. Clarence E. Hill Jr., "Undoubtedly, Romo Can't Afford to Drop the Ball," *Fort Worth Star-Telegram*, September 9, 2007, 8C.

6. Jim Reeves, "Sack Proves Romo's Vast Improvement at AB is Out of the Bag," *Fort Worth Star-Telegram*, September 10, 2007, 1DD and 5DD; Mac Engel, "His

Price Keeps Going Up," *Fort Worth Star-Telegram*, October 1, 2007, 5DD; and "Tony Romo," *Pro Football Reference*, https://www.pro-football-reference.com/players/R/RomoTo00/gamelog/2007/.

7. Jim Reeves, "Romo Did Everything Wrong, Then Proved He Was a Winner," *Fort Worth Star-Telegram*, October 9, 2007, 1DD and 4DD.

8. "New England Patriots at Dallas Cowboys—October 14, 2007," *Pro Football Reference*, https://www.pro-football-reference.com/box-scores/200710140dal.htm.

9. Mac Engel, "Romo Unchanged by Contract," *Fort Worth Star-Telegram*, November 5, 2007, 5DD.

10. Rick Herrin, "Crayton's Return Good for Two TD Receptions," *Fort Worth Star-Telegram*, November 30, 2007, 4DD and "Dallas Cowboys at Detroit Lions: December 9, 2007," https://www.pro-football-reference.com/boxscores/200712090det.htm.

11. Randy Galloway, "With Their QB Stumbling, the Cowboys Fell Like Dominos," *Fort Worth Star-Telegram*, December 17, 2007, 1DD and 6DD and Jennifer Floyd Engel, "Ghost of Decembers Past Look to be Haunting Cowboys Again," *Fort Worth Star-Telegram*, December 17, 2007, 1DD and 5DD.

12. "Tony Romo," *Pro Football Reference*, https://www.pro-football-reference.com/players/R/RomoTo00/gamelog/2007/; and "2007 Dallas Cowboys Statistics & Players," https://www.pro-football-reference.com/teams/dal/2007.htm. See also Newy Scruggs, "In My Opinion," *Fort Worth Star-Telegram*, January 12, 2008, Z2.

13. "Divisional Round-New York Giants at Dallas Cowboys—January 13, 2007," https://www.pro-football-reference.com/

boxscores/200801130dal.htm.

14. David Thomas, "Say Adios, Vaqueros; The Super Season is No Mas," *Fort Worth Star-Telegram*, January 14, 2008, 2DD; Jim Reeves, "Lessons, If Not Playoff Victories, Piling Up for Cowboys' Young Quarterback," *Fort Worth Star-Telegram*, January 14, 2008, 1DD and 7DD; and Clarence E. Hill Jr., Mac Engel, and Rick Herrin, "Good, Bad and Ugly Ending," *Fort Worth Star-Telegram*, January 16, 2008, 6D.

15. "Romo's Father Diagnosed with Prostate Cancer," *ESPN News*, October 12, 2007, https://www. espn.com/nfl/news/story?id=3059911. See also Peter Jackel, "Romo Stays True to His Roots," *The Journal Times*, June 23, 2008, https://journal-times.com/sports/jackel-romo-stays-true-to-roots/article_a8a8a08e-4e35-5952-a7fb-31e69feeb70e.html.

16. Jennifer Floyd Engel, "After Sunday, Eli Has the Ring of Greatness," *Fort Worth Star-Telegram*, February 5, 2008, 2D.

17. Gil LeBreton, "Impressive Rise, But Romo Has to Shed Playoff Albatross," *Fort Worth Star-Telegram*, July 18, 2008, 1D and 8D; and Newy Scruggs, "Romo Confident Best Days Around Corner," *Fort Worth Star-Telegram*, July 19, 2008, 2D.

18. Mac Engel, "Romo's Homecoming Good Enough to Win," *Fort Worth Star-Telegram*, September 22, 2008, 5DD; "Dallas Cowboys at Green Bay Packers—September 21, 2008," *Pro Football Reference*, https://www.pro-football-reference. com/boxscores/200809210gnb.htm. See also Brett Christopherson, "Small-Town at Heart," *The Post-Crescent*, September 21, 2008, B1 and B11.

19. Clarence E. Hill Jr., "Loss Leaves Cowboys Searching

for Answers," *Fort Worth Star-Telegram*, October 13, 2008, 4DD. See also "2008 Dallas Cowboys Statistics and Players," *Pro Football Reference*, https://www. pro-football-reference.com/teams/dal/2008.htm.

20.   "Seattle Seahawks at Dallas Cowboys—November 27, 2008," https://www.pro-football-reference.com/box-scores/200811270dal.htm.

21.   Gil LeBreton, "It's Time to Assess How Much Blame Actually Falls on Romo," *Fort Worth Star-Telegram*, December 29, 2008, 1DD and 6DD; Rick Herrin, "Blame Abounds After Embarrassing Defeat" and "Romo Collapses in Shower Following Game," *Fort Worth Star-Telegram*, December 29, 2008, 6DD.

22.   Jim Reeves, "In All Honesty, Romo Still Doesn't Quite Get It," *Fort Worth Star-Telegram*, January 1, 2009, 1D and 7D.

23.   "Dallas Cowboys Single-Season Passing Leaders," *Pro Football Reference*, https://www.pro-football-reference. com/teams/dal/single-season-passing.htm.

24.   Clarence E. Hill Jr., "Confident Cowboys Ride Momentum into Playoffs," *Fort Worth Star-Telegram*, January 4, 2010, 4DD.

25.   Randy Galloway, "Stubborn Jerry Listened, But He Still Needs Playoff Payoff," *Fort Worth Star-Telegram*, January 7, 2010, 1D and 2D, and Jan Hubbard, "December Demons Slain, Romo Confronts Playoff Hex," *Fort Worth Star-Telegram*, January 7, 2010, 1D and 2D.

26.   Charean Williams, "Romo Wants More After Earning First Playoff Win," *Fort Worth Star-Telegram*, January 10, 2010, 10C. See also "Wild Card—Philadelphia Eagles at Dallas Cowboys—January 9, 2010," https://www.pro-football-reference.com/box-scores/201001090dal.htm.

27. Clarence E. Hill Jr., "Old-Fashioned Gunfight: Who'll Be Left Standing?" *Fort Worth Star-Telegram*, January 15, 2010, D1, D2.

28. Charean Williams, "Sack It Up: Vikings Don't Allow Romo to be Romo," *Fort Worth Star-Telegram*, January 18, 2010, 6DD. See also "Divisional Round—Dallas Cowboys at Minnesota Vikings—January 17, 2010." https://www.pro-football-reference.com/box-scores/201001170min.htm.

29. Jennifer Floyd Engel, "Romo Still Cowboys' Best Chance at Getting to Super Bowl," *Fort Worth Star-Telegram*, January 18, 2010, 1D and 2D.

30. Angie Alvarado, "Crockett Man's Life Saved by New Cardiac Procedure," *Palestine Herald-Press*, February 27, 2011, https://www.palestineherald.com/news/local_news/crockett-mans-life-saved-by-new-cardiac-procedure/article_0ece6e77-676f-5abb-b144-5ec110cb6067.html.

31. Charean Williams, "Statistics in Hand, Romo Now Wants That Big Victory," *Fort Worth Star-Telegram*, July 25, 2010, 1C and 9C; and Jennifer Floyd Engel, "Romo Works to Get Better, But He Needs a Little Help," *Fort Worth Star-Telegram*, July 29, 2010, 1D and 8D.

32. Jan Hubbard, "For Openers, Romo Sees 'Great Test' for Cowboys," *Fort Worth Star-Telegram*, September 12, 2010, 9C.

33. Charean Williams, "Hold On! Final Penalty Erases Cowboys' Hope," *Fort Worth Star-Telegram*, September 13, 2010, 6CC; Randy Galloway, "Over-Hyped, Under-Coached . . . and a Season Past the Crossroads," *Fort Worth Star-Telegram*, September 20, 2010, 1CC and 8CC; Jan Hubbard, "Jones' 109-Yard Day Overshadowed by Loss," *Fort Worth Star-Telegram*, October 11,

2010, 5CC; Clarence E. Hill Jr., "The Cowboys Self-Destruct in Another Shocking Defeat," *Fort Worth Star-Telegram*, October 11, 2010, 1CC and 5CC; and Charean Williams, "Interceptions Starting to Take a Toll on Romo," *Fort Worth Star-Telegram*, October 18, 2010, 5CC.

34. "New York Giants at Dallas Cowboys—October 25, 2010," *Pro Football Reference*, https://www.pro-football-reference.com/boxscores/201010250dal.htm. See also Charean Williams, "Romo Could be Sidelined 6–8 Weeks," *Fort Worth Star-Telegram*, October 26, 2010, 5D; Jan Hubbard, "Cowboys Started Off Well, But Things Went Downhill Quickly," *Fort Worth Star-Telegram*, October 26, 2010, 5D; Jose Mendez, "Interceptions Only Taint on Kitna's Relief Stint," *Fort Worth Star-Telegram*, December 13, 2010, 5CC; Clarence E. Hill Jr. and Drew Davidson, "Jones Says Romo Won't Play Again This Season," *Fort Worth Star-Telegram*, December 20, 2010, 6CC; and Jan Hubbard, "With Three Sacks, Ware Winds up Atop NFL Again," *Fort Worth Star-Telegram*, January 3, 2011, 6BB.

35. Michelle Kapusta, "Who Is Tony Romo's Wife, Candice Crawford?" *Showbiz Cheatsheet*, September 8, 2019, https://www.cheatsheet.com/entertainment/who-is-tony-romos-wife-candice-crawford.html/.

36. Charean Williams, "Romo Runs Practice, Fiancée Plans Wedding," *Fort Worth Star-Telegram*, May 24, 2011, 4B, and Mike Ramczyk, "Burlington Native Tony Romo Touches on Packers, Married Life and NFL Lockout," *The Lake Geneva Regional News*, June 30, 2011, 1 and 3.

37. Jennifer Floyd Engel, "A New Belief System," *Fort Worth Star-Telegram*, January 4, 2011, 1B and 2B.

38. Mac Engel, "Maybe Romo Should Start Off by Just

Getting Close," *Fort Worth Star-Telegram*, July 19, 2011, 1B and 10B.

39. Randy Galloway, "Riding on Romo," *Fort Worth Star-Telegram*, August 5, 2011, 1D and 8D.

40. Carlos Mendez, "Romo: Step Up, Young Linemen," *Fort Worth Star-Telegram*, August 31, 2011, 2D.

41. Randy Galloway, "Two Blunders by Romo Make All the Difference," *Fort Worth Star-Telegram*, September 12, 2011, 1DD and 5DD.

42. Charean Williams, "Rib Cracked, But Not Romo's Spirit in Win," *Fort Worth Star-Telegram*, September 19, 2011, 5BB.

43. Todd Archer, "Tony Romo's Heritage Always Close By," *ESPN News*, September 22, 2011, https://www.espn.com/nfl/story/_/id/7004118/tony-romo-family-him-every-step-way.

44. Charean Williams, "With the Wraps Off, Romo Can Joke About Perfection," *Fort Worth Star-Telegram*, November 14, 2011, 7B, and "Romo Nearly Flawless vs. Bucs," *Fort Worth Star-Telegram*, December 18, 2011, 3C.

45. Charean Williams, "Romo's Bruised Hand Best News for Cowboys," *Fort Worth Star-Telegram*, December 25, 2011, 5C.

46. Clarence E. Hill Jr., "Firm Belief," *Fort Worth Star-Telegram*, December 29, 2011, 1C and 2C.

47. "Dallas Cowboys at New York Giants—January 1, 2012," *Pro Football Reference* https://www.pro-football-reference.com/boxscores/201201010nyg.htm.

48. Gil LeBreton, "Cowboys Are What They Are, a Simple Pretender," *Fort Worth Star-Telegram*, January 2, 2012, 1C and 7C; Charean Williams, "Romo Won't Blame Injury for Pain of Loss," *Fort Worth Star-Telegram*, January 2, 2012, 7C; and Carlos Mendez, "Ware

Finishes Half-Sack Short of 20 for Year," *Fort Worth Star-Telegram*, January 2, 2012, 18C.

49.   Clarence E. Hill Jr., "Varsity Letters," *Fort Worth Star-Telegram*, January 5, 2012, 4C.

CHAPTER 8

1.   "2011 Dallas Cowboys Statistics and Players," *Pro Football Reference*, https://www.pro-football-reference.com/teams/dal/2011.htm.

2.   "Briefs: Golf," *Fort Worth Star-Telegram*, February 8, 2012, 7C, and Randy Galloway, "Romo's Good, but He's Not in Eli's League," *Fort Worth Star-Telegram*, February 9, 2012, 1C and 3C.

3.   Clarence E. Hill Jr., "Jones Says Callahan Will Make Offensive Line Better," *Fort Worth Star-Telegram*, February 25, 2012, 1C and 2C; Carlos Mendez, "Garrett: Age, Salary Cap Concerns Drove Kosier Cut," *Fort Worth Star-Telegram*, March 25, 2012, 5C; and "2011 Dallas Cowboys Statistics and Players," *Pro Football Reference*, https://www.pro-football-reference.com/teams/dal/2011.htm.

4.   Clarence E. Hill Jr., "As Good As It Gets?", *Fort Worth Star-Telegram*, February 29, 2012, 1C and 5C; "It's a Boy for Tony and Candice Romo," *Fort Worth Star-Telegram*, April 11, 2012, A1; and Mike Ramczyk, "Burlington Native, NFL Star Tony Romo Returns Home," *Lake Geneva Regional News*, June 28, 2012, 1 and 3.

5.   Mac Engel, "It Can't Be the Same Old Story," *Fort Worth Star-Telegram*, December 30, 2012, 1C and 4C.

6.   Randy Galloway, "Romo, Cowboys Still Doing What They Do Best . . . Fail," *Fort Worth Star-Telegram*, December 31, 2012, 1C and 6C; and Clarence E. Hill Jr., "Grading the Cowboys," *Fort Worth Star-Telegram*,

January 6, 2013, 8C.

7.   Clarence E. Hill Jr., "Cowboys Relieve Cap Pressure with Moves," March 1, 2013, 3C; "5 Things to Watch in Free Agency," March 10, 2013, C1 and C5; "Cowboys Release LB Connor to Fit Cap," *Fort Worth Star-Telegram,* March 12, 2013, C1 and C3; and Charean Williams, "Free Agency Doesn't Always Get Teams What They Pay," *Fort Worth Star-Telegram*, March 14, 2013, 3C.

8.   Randy Galloway, "Romo Should Have Gone 'Brady,'" *Fort Worth Star-Telegram*, March 14, 2013, 1C and 3C.

9.   Clarence E. Hill Jr. and Charean Williams, "Cowboys Sign Romo for Six Years," *Fort Worth Star-Telegram*, March 30, 2013, 1C and 2C.

10.   "Denver Broncos at Dallas Cowboys—October 6, 2013," *Pro Football Reference*, https://www.pro-football-reference.com/boxscores/201310060dal.htm.

11.   Carlos Mendez, "Cowboys Haven't Lost Confidence in Romo," *Fort Worth Star-Telegram*, December 22, 2013, 4C.

12.   Clarence E. Hill Jr., "Late Heroics by Romo Set Up Critical Finale," *Fort Worth Star-Telegram*, December 23, 2013, 5C; and Gil LeBreton, "Cowboys, Romo Rise from the Grave for One Last Shot," *Fort Worth Star-Telegram*, December 23, 2013, 1C and 6C.

13.   Rowan Kavner, "Tony Romo Out for Rest of Year After Back Surgery," *Dallas Cowboys*, December 27, 2013, https://www.dallascowboys.com/news/tony-romo-out-for-rest-of-year-after-back-surgery-345741; Charean Williams, "With Orton, Cowboys Not About to Concede," *Fort Worth Star-Telegram*, December 26, 2013, 1C and 6C; and Clarence E. Hill Jr., "Romo's Out, Orton's Up," *Fort Worth Star-Telegram*, December 29, 2013, 1C and 8C; "It's Déjà vu for Dallas: 8–8 and

No Playoffs," *Fort Worth Star-Telegram*, December 30, 2013, 1A; and "Final Grades," *Fort Worth Star-Telegram*, January 5, 2014, 6C.

14. S. L. Price, "Why Ya Gotta Hate?"

15. Carlos Mendez, "Owner Jones Says Romo on Track After Back Surgery," *Fort Worth Star-Telegram*, January 21, 2014, 2C; Mac Engel, "Jerry's Mantra of Change Should Include Drafting QB," *Fort Worth Star-Telegram*, February 13, 2014, 1C and 3C; Clarence E. Hill Jr., "Romo Hasn't Thrown But Is Ahead in Rehab," *Fort Worth Star-Telegram*, March 26, 2014, 5C; and Charean Williams, "Focus Hits 2 Cowboys Rookies," *Fort Worth Star-Telegram*, May 22, 2014, 2C.

16. Clarence E. Hill Jr., "Romo Questionable Against Chargers," *Fort Worth Star-Telegram*, August 1, 2014, 1C and 8C; Charean Williams, "Romo Will Skip Preseason Opener," *Fort Worth Star-Telegram*, August 4, 2014, 12C; "Caution Flag Still Out on Romo," August 19, 2014, 2C; and "Team Stands by Quarterback," September 8, 2014, 16C.

17. Charean Williams, "Romo Hurt, But Returns," *Fort Worth Star-Telegram*, October 28, 2014, 3C, and Clarence E. Hill Jr., "Substandard," *Fort Worth Star-Telegram*, November 3, 2014, 1C.

18. Clarence E. Hill Jr., "Like it or Not, Romo Still Key to Success," *Fort Worth Star-Telegram*, November 11, 2014, 1C and 4C.

19. Gil LeBreton, "After Five Years in the Wilderness, the Playoff Drought is Over," *Fort Worth Star-Telegram*, December 22, 2014, 1C; Charean Williams, "Romo for League MVP? It's Worth a Closer Look," *Fort Worth Star-Telegram*, December 22, 2014, 7C; and Joseph Zucker, "NFL MVP 2014–2015: Winner, Voting Results

and Twitter Reaction," *Bleacher Report*, January 31, 2015, https://bleacherreport.com/articles/2349593-nfl-mvp-2014-15-winner-voting-results-and-twitter-reaction.

20. David Flores, "'We Are So Blessed': Grandparents Proud of Romo's Success," *News Taco*, January 2, 2015, https://newstaco.com/2015/01/02/we-are-so-blessed-grandparents-proud-of-romos-success/.

21. Clarence E. Hill Jr., "Cowboys Take Down Lions," *Fort Worth Star-Telegram*, January 5, 2015, 4CC; Mac Engel, "Faith Was Rewarded as Romo and Garrett 'Share a Moment,'" *Fort Worth Star-Telegram*, January 5, 2015, 1CC; and "Cowboys Storm Back, Then Hold Off Lions," *ESPN News*, January 5, 2015, https://www.espn.com/nfl/game/_/gameId/400749514.

22. Charean Williams, "Romo Plays Through Pain to Give Cowboys a Chance," *Fort Worth Star-Telegram*, January 12, 2015, 4CC; Mac Engel, "Cowboys Should Only Blame Themselves," *Fort Worth Star-Telegram*, January 12, 2015, 1CC and 4CC; and Gil LeBreton, "This Judgement Call Fails the Eyeball Test," *Fort Worth Star-Telegram*, January 12, 2015, 1CC and 3CC.

23. Clarence E. Hill Jr., "Final Grades," *Fort Worth Star-Telegram*, January 18, 2015, 5C. See also Bob Braun, "Watt Picks, Recovers, Dances," *Fort Worth Star-Telegram*, January 26, 2015, 2B.

24. Drew Davison, "A Question for the Aged," *Fort Worth Star-Telegram*, July 28, 2015, 1B and 3B; Charean Williams, "Cowboys Threaten Mincey with Fines," *Fort Worth Star-Telegram*, July 30, 2015, 12B; Drew Davison, "Hot Routes," *Fort Worth Star-Telegram*, August 3, 2015, 10B; and Charean Williams, "Hot Routes," *Fort Worth Star-Telegram*, August 6, 2015, 12B.

25. Clarence E. Hill Jr., "Health Top Priority for Cowboys,"

Fort Worth Star-Telegram, August 26, 2015, 3E.

26. "Cowboys Replay," *Fort Worth Star-Telegram*,
September 14, 2015, 5B; Drew Davison, "Romo's
Flawless Fourth-Quarter Play Led Way," *Fort Worth
Star-Telegram*, September 14, 2015, 7B; David Thomas,
"Romo Mojo," *Fort Worth Star-Telegram*, September 16,
2015, 1B; and Gil LeBreton, "Heroic Romo Writes Still
Another Happy Ending for the Cowboys," *Fort Worth
Star-Telegram*, September 14, 2015, 1B and 7B.

27. "Cowboys Replay," *Fort Worth Star-Telegram*, September
21, 2015, 5B; and Mac Engel, "Weeden Needs a
Lot of Help to Keep This Season Afloat," *Fort Worth
Star-Telegram*, September 21, 2015, 1B and 7B.

28. Randy Galloway, "Garrett Should Try to Get Fired," *Fort
Worth Star-Telegram*, November 22, 2015, 1C and 2C;
and Clarence E. Hill Jr., "Return to Contender?" *Fort
Worth Star-Telegram*, November 23, 2015, 1B and 5B.

29. Clarence E. Hill Jr., "Breaking Down the Quarters," *Fort
Worth Star-Telegram*, November 27, 2015, 6B; Charean
Williams, "Romo Likely Done as QB, Team Can't
Catch a Break," *Fort Worth Star-Telegram*, 7B; and Drew
Davison, "With Romo Out for Year, Cowboys' Year a
Bust," *Fort Worth Star-Telegram*, November 29, 2015, 1B
and 5B; and Charean Williams, "Romo Vows Best Years
Are Ahead," *Fort Worth Star-Telegram*, January 5, 2016,
1B and 2B.

30. Mac Engel, "Jerry Jones Too Old for a Rookie
Quarterback," *Fort Worth Star-Telegram*, March 1, 2016,
1B and 2B; Charean Williams, "Boykin Throws, Catches;
Doctson Draws Crowd," *Fort Worth Star-Telegram*,
April 1, 2016, 1B and 3B; Clarence E. Hill Jr., "Triplets
Version 2.0," *Fort Worth Star-Telegram*, April 29, 2016,
1B and 9B; and Drew Davison, "Prescott Seen as Starter

Material," *Fort Worth Star-Telegram*, May 2, 2016.

31. Mac Engel, "This is the Beginning of the End for Romo," *Fort Worth Star-Telegram*, August 28, 2016, 1C and 9C; and Clarence E. Hill Jr., "Down, and Now Out," *Fort Worth Star-Telegram*, August 28, 2016, 1C and 9C.

32. Charean Williams, "Elliott Hurdling, Running Over Foes," *Fort Worth Star-Telegram*, November 4, 2016, 2B; and Clarence E. Hill Jr., "Cowboys QB Romo Shows Grace in Accepting Backup Role to Prescott," *Fort Worth Star-Telegram*, November 19, 2016, 12A; Mac Engel, "Romo Needs to Play One More Time for Cowboys," January 1, 2017, 1C and 4C; and Clarence E. Hill Jr., "Breaking Down the Quarters," *Fort Worth Star-Telegram*, January 2, 2017, 6B.

33. Clarence E. Hill Jr., "Tony Romo Waiting Game Continues," *Fort Worth Star-Telegram*, March 22, 2017, 3B; and "Romo Warm to Jones, Still Cold to Garrett," *Fort Worth Star-Telegram*, April 7, 2017, B2.

34. Clarence E. Hill Jr., "Family Was the X Factor in Romo's Retirement," *Fort Worth Star-Telegram*, April 5, 2017, 1B and 4B; and Charean Williams, "Romo Leaves NFL for TV," *Fort Worth Star-Telegram*, April 5, 2017, 1B and 4B.

35. Jay Busbee, "Tony Romo Wins High Praise for His Broadcast Debut," *Yahoo! Sports*, September 10, 2017, https://sports.yahoo.com/tony-romo-wins-high-praise -broadcast-debut-195933690.html.

CONCLUSION

1. Jim Gorant, "The Case for . . . Fewer Cowboys," *Sports Illustrated*, April 17, 2017, https://vault.si.com/ vault/2017/04/17/case-fewer-cowboys.

2. Phil Mushnick, "Phil Simms Era at CBS Wasn't Supposed to End Like This," *New York Post*, April 6,

2017, https://nypost.com/2017/04/06/phil-simms-era-
at-cbs-wasnt-supposed-to-end-like-this/.

3.   Jason Berman, "Why is Phil Simms Being Replaced
on CBS? Tony Romo Takes Over as New NFL Lead
Analyst," *MIC*, April 5, 2017, https://www.mic.com/
articles/173250/why-is-phil-simms-being-replaced-on-
cbs-tony-romo-takes-over-as-new-nfl-lead-analyst.

4.   Drew Davison, "Romo Falls Short in U.S. Open Bid,"
Fort Worth Star-Telegram, May 9, 2017, 1B and 4B.

5.   Drew Davison, "Romo Gets Rave Reviews for His Work
in CBS Broadcast Booth," *Fort Worth Star-Telegram*,
September 11, 2017, B5; and Stefan Stevenson, "Romo's
Success Comes as No Surprise to Sham," *Fort Worth
Star-Telegram*, November 3, 2017, 1B and 4B.

6.   Stefan Stevenson, "Romo Shows Off Broadcasting
Skill in AT&T Stadium Return," *Fort Worth
Star-Telegram*, November 6, 2017, B4; Drew Davison,
"Cowboys Chasing Playoffs as Chargers Visit on
Thanksgiving," *Fort Worth Star-Telegram*, November
23, 2017, B4; and *Pro Football Reference*, "Kansas
City Chiefs at Dallas Cowboys—November 5,
2017," https://www.pro-football-reference.com/box-
scores/201711050dal.htm.

7.   Drew Davison, "As Tony Romo Readies to Call AFC
Game, Does He Miss His Playing Days?" *Fort Worth
Star-Telegram*, January 20, 2018, A5.

8.   Drew Davison, "Tony Romo's Latest Golf Adventure is
Big-Time," *Fort Worth Star-Telegram*, February 8, 2018,
2B; "Tony Romo Gets Playing Partners for PGA Tour
Event," *Fort Worth Star-Telegram*, March 21, 2018, 8B;
"Tony Romo to Make Another Bid for U.S. Open,"
Fort Worth Star-Telegram, April 28, 2018, 6B; and
Associated Press, "Romo Misses Out on Local US Open

Qualifying," *Fort Worth Star-Telegram*, May 1, 2018, 2B.

9. Clarence E. Hill Jr., "He's 'Romo-stradamus' of Super Bowl LIII, But Romo is Mum on Cowboys' Future," *Fort Worth Star-Telegram*, January 31, 2019, 1B.

10. Jabari Young, "Tony Romo Reaches Historic, Long-Term Deal with CBS Sports, Source Says," *CNBC*, February 28, 2020, https://www.cnbc.com/2020/02/28/tony-romo-reaches-historic-long-term-deal-with-cbs-spor ts-source-says.html. See also Reece Kelley Graham, "New Details About Tony Romo's CBS Extension Reveal Total Worth of $180 Million, Report Says," *Dallas News*, March 2, 2020, https://www.dallasnews. com/sports/cowboys/2020/02/29/tony-romos-new-contract-with-cbs-makes-him-the-highest-paid-nfl-analyst-in-tv-history/.

11. Peter Jackel and Adam Rogan, "Burlington High School's Football Field Might be Renamed to 'Tony Romo Field,'" *The Journal Times*, February 25, 2020, https://www.kenoshanews.com/sports/burlington-high-schools-football-field-might-be-renamed-to-tony-romo-field/article_42622a15-74f3-5fac-97e1-703b3dcc6b97.html. Email correspondence from Peter Jackel to Jorge Iber, May 27, 2021. Copy of email in author's possession. Drew Davison, "Tony Romo Makes the Ballot for 2021 Hall of Fame Class," *Fort Worth Star-Telegram*, June 17, 2020, 3B; Clarence E. Hill Jr., "Romo to College Football Hall of Fame," *Fort Worth Star-Telegram*, January 12, 2021, 3B.

12. Ty Schalter, "Tony Romo Was a Good QB in an Era of Great Ones," *FiveThirtyEight*, April 5, 2017, https:// fivethirtyeight.com/features/tony-romo-was-a-good-qb-in-an-era-of-great-ones/.

13. "Ramiro R. Romo, 1933–2020," *The Journal*

Times, October 28, 2020, https://www.leg-acy.com/us/obituaries/journaltimes/name/ramiro-romo-obituary?pid=197009606.

14.   Jon Kozlowski, "Tony Romo Made His Family's American Dream Come True by Playing for the Dallas Cowboys," *Sportscasting*, July 14, 2020, https://www.sportscasting.com/tony-romo-made-his-familys-american-dream-come-true-by-playing-for-the-dallas-cowboys/.

CPSIA information can be obtained
at www.ICGtesting.com
Printed in the USA
LVHW111807171022
730893LV00004B/495

9 781682 831588